The Case for Physician Assisted Suicide

Other titles in the Pandora Soapbox series:

The Case Against Hysterectomy
The Case For Taking the Date Out of Rape

The Case for

Physician Assisted Suicide

SHEILA MCLEAN AND ALISON BRITTON

An Imprint of HarperCollins*Publishers*

Pandora
An Imprint of HarperCollins*Publishers*
77–85 Fulham Palace Road,
Hammersmith, London W6 8JB

1160 Battery Street,
San Francisco, California 94111-1213
Published by Pandora 1997

10 9 8 7 6 5 4 3 2 1

A catalogue record for this book
is available from the British Library

ISBN 0 04 440983 4

179.7
mcl
&.1

Printed in Great Britain by
Caledonian International Book Manufacturing, Glasgow

This is dedicated to the ones we love

Contents

Acknowledgements

There are many people to whom we wish to express our gratitude. First, and most importantly, to the Voluntary Euthanasia Society of Scotland, whose financial support enabled the original research project to be undertaken. We are also grateful to them for accepting *ab initio* that, in the way of academic research, we started the project with no clear idea of what our conclusions would be. That these independent conclusions accord with the aims of voluntary euthanasia is a tribute to the strength of the arguments which we analysed. In addition, it must be noted that it was the strength of these arguments which led us to rewrite the report in its present form, freed from the constraints of pure academic presentation and motivated by our convictions concerning the need for the arguments themselves to be given a wider airing.

We were fortunate to obtain assistance from a number of other individuals and organizations at various stages of our research, although it must be said that the fact that they were willing to help should in no way be taken as implying that they agree with our conclusions. All of the following deserve special mention:

Mr Angus Stewart QC

Professor J. M. Thomson, Regius Professor of Law at Glasgow University

Colleagues in the Department of Behavioural Sciences at Glasgow University, particularly Dr K. Mullan

The team working on *Frontline Scotland* at BBC Scotland, who commissioned the public opinion poll

Staff at the Hemlock Society in Eugene, Oregon for their generosity with both time and library resources

Cheryl Smith for time and inspiration

System 3 for their outstandingly professional preparation and analysis of the data from both the opinion poll and the survey.

In addition, Bill Black was his usual helpful self in more ways than we can list. Last, but not least, we are indebted to Mitch Britton for being a computer wizard!

Sheila A. M. McLean
Alison Britton
Glasgow University
St Andrew's Day 1996

Introduction

Death is sometimes a small victory
Chinese Proverb

That death can be a triumph is a notion which can trace its history back over centuries. It is, perhaps, only in the last century, with its combination of scientific advance and rising expectations, that death has come to be so feared. That this is so may well be a result of the fact that we live in an illusion of control. The major advances in science and medicine have brought both death and increased life expectancy. Science's awesome power to destroy led to our demand for control and perpetuated the myth that such control was feasible. Recent history might suggest that our capacity to shape our environment is little more than illusion, yet in a century where the individual sees him- or herself as the centre of the Universe, this illusion is both necessary and predictable. At the same time, medical (and social) advances have encouraged the view that death can be, if not avoided, at least delayed.

Yet, for many, control has a wider aspect. Certainly, many if
not all of us would wish to extend life for as long as that life brings
something good with it. But medicine can only do so much, and the
time comes when some people judge that the quality of their life is
insufficiently good to justify its being sustained. When care, medication
and comfort no longer suffice to make each day a blessing, or even
tolerable, it is clear that many will feel that the right to control their
own life should in justice include the right to manage their death.

Of course, there is enormous resistance to this claim. Some
comes from the tenets of religion, which believe life to be a non-
returnable gift from God. Yet more comes from those who fear that
self-control will become public control. And, of course, the law sees
itself as the upholder of traditional values, such as the sanctity of all
life, and is, in its rhetoric at least, firmly wedded to the protection of
each of these lives.

No purpose is served by belittling people's firmly held religious or
moral views, and we have no intention of making such an attempt.
What can, however, rationally be addressed are the prohibitions on
achieving one's own 'small victory'. Of course, suicide is an option,
now decriminalized, but there are those who, for emotional, practical
or contextual reasons, cannot kill themselves. Many of these will be
patients, confined to institutions or without access to the means with
which to take their own life. Prisoners of a system which, albeit for
the best of motives, has rendered drugs as safe as possible and offers
little scope for self-willed decisions, they are condemned to be
disenfranchised at one of the most significant stages of their life –
namely its ending.

Fear of death, of oblivion, is a phenomenon encouraged by the
hopes held out by modern medicine and one which doubtless both
informs societies' attitudes to those who claim the right to choose
death over life and fuels the empty rhetoric which characterizes the
legal approach to death and dying. As will become evident, the law is

at best ambivalent and at worst disingenuous in its approach to end-of-life decisions. In many countries, criminal courts cannot impose death on a convicted criminal, but in these same countries, civil courts in dealing with handicapped neonates or people in persistent vegetative state are given the power to make decisions which result in precisely the same outcome. The significance of this is not that we should restore the power to criminal courts, but rather that decisions about someone else's life are taken at the lesser standard of proof required by the civil law. Courts endorsing decisions which result in death are required to find that the evidence points in that direction only on the balance of probabilities, and not on the stricter criminal law test of 'beyond reasonable doubt'.

Of course, the response to this might be that the civil courts are authorizing 'letting die', and not 'killing' – an argument which, as will be seen later, has served to obfuscate what is actually happening: third parties (those who are allowed to let someone die) are in fact participating in the death of a third person, whether or not their consciences can be squared by clinging to the disingenuous doctrine of acts and omissions. Moreover, often these decisions are taken in the absence of any input from the person whose life is at stake.

The paradox is that, if a competent and considered request for assistance in dying is made by the person whose life is **for him or her** no longer more of a benefit than a burden, in most – although as will be seen, not all – countries this request will be denied, and anyone who assists in that death will be guilty of a criminal offence.

In reviewing the arguments for and against permitting people to seek assistance in their death, it becomes clear that the strength of the arguments in favour is considerable. Equally, the weaknesses in the arguments against are clear.

This book does not seek to force death on the unwilling – there is no slippery slope in accepting the arguments in favour of choice. Nor, although it concentrates on physician assistance, would the arguments contained in it require a doctor's participation. Rather, it is an attempt dispassionately to evaluate the competing arguments which, inevitably in view of their strength, come down on the side of those who wish lawfully to gain help in dying.

The book is based on a report prepared by the authors, and takes account of both intellectual arguments and evidence from individuals, doctors and others. What the latter shows is that attitudes are changing. The fear of death is being supplanted by the fear of unwanted life. Our premise is that, unless it is clear that real danger lurks in taking account of the intellectual and practical realities of the contemporary drive towards increased control of dying, it is no longer those who seek its legalization who must make their case – instead, those who would deny this right to others must justify theirs.

Why Not Assisted Suicide?

We have made a covenant with death
Isaiah 22:16

One thing is clear – we must all die. Not even the miracles of modern medicine can prevent the inevitable. Yet, of course, life is our most precious possession because, ultimately, it is all we have. It is scarcely surprising, then, that people strive to avoid the end and that a thirst for life is common. But however hard it is to accept, there are some people who prefer to end their lives, because of despair, distress or disease.

Perhaps strangely in a book which is making the case in favour of assisted suicide, we have chosen to begin with a review of the arguments against permitting it. Before doing this it is necessary to define assisted suicide, not least because it can be distinguished from that other highly emotive topic, euthanasia. Although it is conceded that the arguments for assisted suicide could also be used for voluntary euthanasia, there are differences between the two. While voluntary euthanasia requires a third party to carry out the act leading to death, assisted suicide 'involves an individual taking his or her own life **with the help of another**. The circumstances in which patients may request assistance to commit suicide are those where there is a desire to end suffering and maintain control of personal destiny, but this is impossible without help'[1]. Because assisted suicide is a deliberate and personal act, we have chosen to focus on it as the clearer example of self-governance.

Like it or not, although the law in most jurisdictions (but not all) outlaws the provision of the means to help another person to die, it is clear that aid in dying is provided. What is less clear is the extent to which this is happening, partly because of the fear of prosecution which would follow an admission and partly because death is traditionally seen as a private matter. However, there is research which suggests that the incidence of aid in dying is reasonably significant. In 1993, for example, it was estimated that as many as 6,000 of the deaths occurring daily in the US may have involved third-party assistance.[2] Evidence from the Netherlands suggests that about 0.3 per cent of deaths over any given year were the result of physician assisted suicide (and this in addition to the number of deaths resulting from voluntary euthanasia).[3] In 1995, Osgood reported that the retired US physician, Dr Jack Kevorkian, had assisted 21 people to commit suicide; this number has increased since then without a single successful prosecution.[4]

So, although it is against the law in many countries, it does happen. Of course, the fact that it is going on is not in itself an argument for changing the law to accommodate it, but does suggest that sufficient numbers of people want to be allowed to have assistance in dying, and that there are a number of people who will willingly – even if reluctantly – provide it. Our own survey of the public in Scotland showed a clear majority in favour of being allowed to seek help in dying, a result which, as will be seen below, is mirrored in other countries. Also, our survey of doctors and pharmacists throughout the UK showed a majority in favour of legal change, and surveys elsewhere have demonstrated that increasing numbers of doctors (and others) are willing to help when a competent request for assistance has been made. (*For further information on this, see Chapter 5.*)

Naturally, we accept that this is at best anecdotal evidence, but it is none the less repeated so often in different cultures that it must carry a little more weight than might otherwise be attributed to it. Despite this, however, there are many people for whom the idea of a controlled or contrived death is anathema, and their views must also be taken into account. However, it must be said at the outset that the case for assisted suicide depends on liberty, not on coercion. For those who disapprove of an enabled death, there is no argument presented here which would force them into accepting it for themselves. Significantly, however, if we adhere to their perspective, then we deny others the respect which their position should also command.

Perhaps the strongest, and certainly the most often used, argument against assisted suicide is the sanctity of life. This is a common theme of objectors, based on either religious or moral commitments. Support for this approach comes from a variety of sources. It is the mantra of most courts that their fundamental commitment is to the sanctity of life, although it must be said that this rhetoric is not always followed in practice. In effect, the courts' commitment is a negative rather than a positive one, as is shown by the fact that they will endorse the competent decision of a patient to refuse life-saving treatment[5] and will sometimes permit the selective non-treatment of handicapped infants.[6] In each of these cases, the court permits death to occur by allowing other precepts, such as autonomy or quality of life, to prevail. This shows that the courts are not prepared to **force** life on people. Thus, while they may see themselves as acting to ensure, as Giesen says, that '... the sanctity of human life, and, thus, respect for human life is maintained against the tide of ethical relativism and moral decline ...',' they none the less expressly concede that life for some people may not be preferable to death.

The sanctity of life approach, then, implies no coercion, although it is often interpreted by its adherents as being sufficient justification to validate forcing others to live when they would prefer not to.

Equally, this argument might encapsulate one based on the concept of a 'right to life'. This right is taken to be inalienable – that is, one which cannot be taken away by others. But the same point about negativity can be made: As CeloCruz points out, '... it is not at all clear why the inalienability of my right to life, per se, prevents me from killing myself.'[8] The rhetoric of the right to life would not, therefore, prevent people from suicide, it would only prevent others from killing them against, or without reference to, their own preferences. In effect, it is a right not to be murdered and certainly does not of itself argue against the existence of a right to choose to be helped to die.

Nor does it imply that everyone always has a duty to save a life. As Gillon points out:

Medicine, law and everyday morality distinguish clearly between a strong universal though prima facie prohibition on killing and a very much more equivocal attitude to letting die. The assumption underlying this general approach seems to be that all of us owe a strong prima facie duty to all others not to kill each other but that we may or may not, depending on the circumstances and the relationships involved, owe a duty to each other to preserve each other's lives.[9]

What we can say about the sanctity of life argument is that it stands firmly against the wrongful killing of others; to that extent it is indeed a cornerstone of civilized society. What it does not do, however, is provide a justification for forcing people to continue to live. Having said this, and given that even the hospice movement in its evidence to the House of Lords Select Committee on Medical Ethics[10] conceded that 'in our moral framework there are no absolute principles which can never be overridden by others ...',[11] there are still some who would argue that the sanctity of life argument has a value which must always dominate.

The argument is probably more likely to be rooted in religious than secular ethics – namely, that life is a gift from God and can only be terminated by that higher being. In this framework both suicide and assisted suicide would infringe the ethic. We have neither the interest nor the intention to challenge those for whom the sanctity of life is a positive obligation, but their objections must also be seen as personal, and to this extent, while **they** may adhere to this principle, it is not clear from where the authority to impose it on others actually derives.

There may be additional, non-religious, objections to the endorsement or legalization of assisted suicide which relate to what legalization would imply about the value of life itself. In other words, some may argue that the phenomenon of choosing one's own death would have repercussions for us all, and that these would be sufficiently grave to justify interfering in the liberty of others. Certainly, rights may come into conflict, and even if it were agreed that none of us need be bound by the views of others, however firmly held, the effect of people being free to make certain choices might impact on the wider community and reduce the strength of individuals' right to act as they choose.

Reno,[12] for example, addresses this question from the perspective of the state's interest in preserving life. This interest extends both to the person who wishes to choose his or her own death and beyond to the community of which the person is a part: 'Those who are concerned about the suicidant contend that if suicide and assisted suicide were permitted, society would become increasingly indifferent to the value of life. This indifference, in turn, would eventually lead to the elimination of those whom society deems undesirable or unworthy of scarce medical resources.'[13]

Obviously there are some individuals and groups for whom this warning has particular resonance – for example, the elderly, the disabled, and so on. For them the fear that this scenario would come about is both pressing and real. However, those who argue from this perspective miss a fundamental point: The case for assisted suicide is a case **for** choice, not for its removal. A person's freedom to do X does not mean that others will have X forced upon them.

Indeed, we already have evidence that this argument does not work. Current laws permit competent adults to choose death by refusing medical treatment, and permit, as has already been said, carers to decide that the life of a handicapped infant should not be saved. All of these are legal endorsements of passive euthanasia or what Glover[14] has called 'non-voluntary euthanasia'. That the law will not step in to criminalize these decisions shows that we already do accept that some lives are not worth living, even in situations where this conclusion is reached by others, not by the person concerned. Two things need to be said about this conclusion. First that, when an adult is allowed to choose not to survive, we are demonstrating a respect for autonomy or self-determination over the sanctity of life. Second, that passive non-voluntary euthanasia has not led to the wholesale slaughter of others envisaged by those who hold out nightmare scenarios. In fact, there is no evidence that choices for death, however controversial, have an adverse effect on society, nor that they weaken our general commitment to preserving life.

In the case of the handicapped infant, it must be clear that the decision which is being taken is not one based on autonomy but rather on quality of life. In one UK case,[15] for example, where a continuation of treatment was required by the court, this decision was reached because the quality of the child's life was not seen to be 'demonstrably awful'. Nevertheless the door has been left open, in this and other countries, to allow in future for lives of poor quality to be ended.

In the case of the adult who refuses treatment, we are allowing the individual him- or herself to make a quality-of-life decision which overrides society's interest in preserving life. But, of course, some would say that there is a big difference between letting someone die and actively colluding in that death. This is what is usually referred to as the acts/omissions distinction. Although not strictly an argument against individual choice, it merits consideration because it is often used to salve the consciences of those who accept the reasoning that death is preferable but who would none the less wish to maintain the somewhat peculiar position that a life may be ended by request only if it is ended in a particular way.

Briefly, what this approach would say is that a person is liable for his or her acts but not for his or her omissions – that there is a moral and legal distinction which can be drawn between them. In a general sense, of course, this is true. I may not kill you (an act), but I have no legal obligation (although arguably I may have a moral one) not to watch you being killed (an omission). However, even if we are comfortable with this distinction, it only holds if there is no pre-existing duty of care. Thus, parents and doctors will be equally liable for their omissions as for their acts, because they have a special duty-based relationship with their children or their patients.

The doctor who permits a patient to refuse life-sustaining treatment or who lets a handicapped infant die cannot, therefore, use this distinction to absolve him- or herself of moral complicity in the death. It may be more comfortable to feel that there is a difference between the two, but technically there is no legal difference and probably no moral one. We already do allow physicians to participate in the death of their patients, although we are more comfortable with one way of doing this than another. However, there is no moral reason to focus on the **manner** in which the outcome is achieved. The fact that doctors may be more comfortable with one form of assistance rather than another does not make any moral difference to the act itself.

There are, of course, other arguments against refusing to permit a choice for death, some of which are specific to medicine and the clinical setting. What if, the question is asked, we decide to die and a cure suddenly becomes available which would have changed our choice? The decision to die, once acted upon, allows no room for back-tracking. While recognizing that this is a genuine concern, it is an argument which can easily be discounted. Advances in medicine simply do not happen overnight. In any event, a person who makes a choice to die will only be making a valid choice if he or she is informed about any new treatment which might be available in the relatively near future – clearly this is likely to form a part of the person's ultimate decision. Indeed, given the fact that most people would intuitively wish to reassure patients, and perhaps would prefer to see them live, there is no doubt that any improved palliation or therapy would clearly, perhaps even forcefully, be brought to their attention.

In any event, for many of those seeking assisted death their condition is already severe, if not terminal, and there is a limit to how much benefit they would gain even if a new treatment became available. There is only so much that medicine can do, and 'There appears to be an upper limit to the number of times any cell can reproduce itself, and modern biologists are beginning to suspect that senescence is built into the biochemical instructions of the living cell and that the ability to divide and reproduce is just as susceptible to metabolic error as all other functions. If this is so, we must regard death as an intrinsic feature of life, and not merely an unavoidable interruption of it.'[16]

But, it might be argued, even if cure is out of the question, there is no need for people to ask for help in dying because palliation is available and successful. The paradigmatic image of the person driven to asking for help to die is that of someone in extreme and unrelievable pain, for whom life is a burden, not a benefit. This deceptively simple argument can, however, also be challenged. In the first place, it may not be pain that triggers the request for aid in dying. For some, suffering is intolerable not because of physical pain but because of other factors. We may suffer without being in pain. The condition(s) which trigger a request for assistance may relate to the indignity of our condition, the emotional problems of coping with it, or any number of other factors which – for the individual concerned – amount to intolerable and unrelievable suffering. Counselling, palliation and other strategies may help, but will not inevitably do so. Indignities may be minimized but not removed.

Of course, in some cases it may well be that the reason for the request for aid in dying **is** severe pain. Undoubtedly, the work of, for example, the hospice movement has resulted in great strides in dealing with the dying, and there is little doubt that, in their own words, 'with modern palliative methods almost all pain can be relieved, and can always be reduced ...'[17] However, even assuming that pain is the primary concern, this statement is honest enough to make it clear that not all pain **can** be successfully controlled. In addition, and again by their own admission, '... occasionally, where all other methods to relieve distress have been tried and failed, sedation ... may be required.'[18] While not doubting their motives, it might be argued that existence in a sedated state might well be one of the very conditions which the sufferer seeks to avoid. It has been said, for example, that 'It is certain that placing dying patients under prolonged and deep anaesthesia would relieve their symptoms. But many experts claim that this practice increasingly being used by hospice physicians today, is virtually the same as killing the patient.

WHY NOT ASSISTED SUICIDE?

Residing in a deep, drug-induced coma while awaiting death can be, from the patient's point of view, no different from death itself.'[19] In any event, even if pain can be relieved by methods short of sedation, the original point remains: it is for the patient and the patient alone to assess the quality of his or her life – and pain, controlled or not, may be only one part of the jigsaw.

Moreover, the impact of the hospice movement on the desire for assisted death needs to be evaluated. The general assumption seems to be that patients who receive hospice care will seldom, if ever, ask for help in dying. If we can manage symptoms, encourage people to talk about their problems and provide high quality care during the dying process, then surely there would be no incentive to die. Seale and Addington-Hall undertook empirical research which led to findings which may come as a surprise to many. Their gentle scepticism of the claim that hospice patients seldom ask for assistance in dying led them to conclude that evidence for this assertion was needed. Whilst agreeing that the hospice movement had made 'an important contribution to the effective and humane care of the dying ...',[20] they concluded that '... the view that hospice care stems the desire of a significant minority of people to die sooner or have euthanasia, receives little support in the findings reported here.'[21] In addition, they discovered that those who were non-professionally involved with hospice patients '... were more likely to feel that an earlier death would have been better'.[22]

These conclusions are highly controversial and challenge much of accepted wisdom. Even if they represent only a small sample, their conclusion that 'the relationship between quality of care and the wish to die earlier is more complex than has hitherto been assumed by those involved in the debate about the legalization of euthanasia...'[23] merits serious consideration.

Few, if any of those whose lives are not intolerable can imagine that death could ever be a preferred option. The instinct for survival is strong, and the temptation may be to dismiss requests for assistance in dying as being in some way the product of psychiatric or psychological disorder. When other people's actions or wishes are puzzling, it is all too common to dismiss them as mad or misguided. Competence to make decisions, then, becomes a further argument against allowing people to make a choice for death.

Certainly, people **do** commit suicide when they are less than rational, and doubtless this will also be true of some of those seeking assistance in dying. But it cannot and should not be assumed that the nature of the request predicts its incompetence. We may be uncomfortable with a wish to die, we may question its rationality and we are certainly entitled to build into the law clear criteria to avoid decisions which are based on a misguided or incompetent request, but the fact that some of the requests may not be competent is not an argument against allowing those which **are** to be acted upon. Ubel puts the case this way: 'Psychiatric diagnoses depend, in part, on lists of behaviours and thoughts. In some diagnoses, feelings of hopelessness and suicidal ideation are criteria for mental illness. This creates a circular chain of diagnostic proof: "Desiring suicide is a sign of mental illness. Mental illness prevents people from being rational. Therefore, desiring suicide is not rational."'[24] Yet he, and many others, would see this as a syllogism which is flawed from the outset by its first presupposition.

In any event, one other analogy is relevant here. Courts have made it clear that patients may refuse life-sustaining treatment on any grounds whatsoever, and that to treat them in the face of such a refusal would be an assault. For the patient whose condition requires an active rather than a passive intervention, the question must be asked why we demand of them the rationality we do not ask of others who equally intend their own death? In addition, the presumption that it is not rational to seek death can be challenged. When the reality of the hopelessness of one's condition is coupled with the physical and/or emotional stresses of living with it, while we might well want to explore the source of the wish to die, we should at the same time avoid the trap of presuming that what to us may seem irrational should automatically be rejected.

Pursuing the question of the cause of the request leads to one further argument which would limit patient choice: namely, the (very real) fear that people's request will stem from pressures put on them by external sources – by greedy relatives or by the burdens associated with meeting healthcare bills, for example. Thus, the request would not be a genuine, valid and intended exercise of self-governance but would rather be the outcome of extraneous factors. There is no doubt that this is a strong argument on several levels. The first, and most obvious, is that people may change their minds if external pressures are removed. In the US this fear has been given real content by the actions of Dr Jack Kevorkian, who has assisted in the death of a number of people. One commentator suggests that he may have '… killed a patient who initially contracted to die but then later pleaded to be taken off Kevorkian's "suicide machine".'[25] If this is so, it conjures up a terrible picture, but it does not constitute an argument for not permitting assisted suicide. Rather it suggests that careful regulation is needed to avoid the involvement of mavericks and to ensure that the request really is enduring. This cannot be done without legal intervention.

Of course, pressure can be more subtle than this. First, there may be well-meaning but misguided pressure from clinicians. In discussing a famous US case concerning Dr Quill and his much publicized assistance of his patient, Diane, in her death, Wesley[26] takes a critical look at the extent to which the physician can ever be non-influential in the ultimate decision. Whilst the doctor may present as merely 'a kind of minimalist mirror or valueless facilitator'[27] of the wishes of the patient, Wesley is concerned that in reality nobody can truly understand the wishes of another and therefore nobody can truly act in a value-free way in carrying out these wishes. This is obviously true in all situations, but it has a particular poignancy when the result is death. Wesley concludes that 'Closely observed, Dr Quill's text itself reveals that he was a powerful actor in his story. With his help, Diane dies a politically correct death, accompanied to her grave by all the rhetoric of patient autonomy and medical egalitarianism that litters our intellectual landscape today, and that distract us from the difficult task of knowing depths of human willing and acting and of trying to preserve life while we do.'[28]

Although this is a powerful analysis, it can also be challenged. We can **never** really know what underlies the choices of others, and we must therefore ask what the purpose of trying to question this particular decision (rather than others) is. Ultimately, the drive to analyse and re-analyse may merely be a disguise for the kind of paternalism which routinely denies the exercise of a choice with which we don't agree. None the less, when coupled with the issues surrounding competence, it is clear that caution is appropriate. However, that caution should extend to respecting other people's decisions as well as to evaluating them for content.

Obviously, however, it might also be thought that there are some groups who are particularly vulnerable to external pressures or whose standing in the community may make them more likely recipients of assistance in dying. Osgood et al,[29] for example, note that most of the people who used Dr Kevorkian's suicide machine were middle-aged women, and that in the US, 'The majority of victims of assisted suicide ... are women.'[30] What is not clear, however, is whether or not this fact can be linked to a gender agenda. There may be any number of other factors which explain this finding, not least because many of the suicides were not conducted in the clinical context but were rather the result of, for example, suicide pacts or what the researchers call 'acquiescent suicide'.[31]

WHY NOT ASSISTED SUICIDE?

Perhaps more obviously, however, the elderly and the
disabled might form groups who could be at risk. Many fear that the
availability of assisted suicide (or euthanasia) would lead the elderly
to request help in dying because they feel themselves to be a burden
or worthless or that their families might benefit, emotionally or
financially, from their early death. Equally, the fact that people are
living longer means that this group will be increasingly represented
as users of healthcare resources. The concern must be that merely
being old might be seen as a reason for seeking death. But the
converse must also be considered. There is evidence that increasing
numbers of elderly people in the US are committing suicide not
because they feel themselves to be a burden, but rather because they
fear being inappropriately kept alive by modern technology.[32] None
the less, Osgood's fears that society may become increasingly 'ageist'
must be taken seriously.

So too must the fears that pressure might be brought to bear on
those who do not fit our notion of 'normality' – namely those who are
in some way disabled. Contemporary society can be just as intolerant
of this group as of the elderly. Miller,[33] for example, talks of society's
'double standards' based on its 'prejudice against persons with
disabilities'.[34] He concludes that 'The current debate over a disabled
person's right to assisted suicide reflects this prejudice.'[35] More subtly,
he suggests, suicide might seem to the able-bodied to be a rational
option if they ever became disabled, making it, he claims, easier to
perceive the suicide of a disabled person as rational, and thus to grant
the expressed wish for help in dying.

Each of these examples, and there are doubtless more, argue for
approaching with caution the legalization of assisted suicide. The
National Council for Hospice and Special Care Services[36] (UK) make a
good point about vulnerability, saying:

*If euthanasia were legalised then society, using doctors as instruments,
would be implying that the deliberate ending of life is acceptable because the*

*loss of that life does not constitute a harm to society and may even be
beneficial to society because that life was of little value. Thus dependent
persons may feel valueless, and may also feel it is their duty to ask for
euthanasia so as not to be a burden.*[37]

The same comments would equally apply to assisted suicide.

However compelling this concern, however, it is also flawed in
one critical respect. Where euthanasia or assisted suicide hinges on a
request being made by the individual, then the only implications
about the worthwhile nature of the life in question are being drawn
by that individual, not by the state. Appropriate legislation, especially
when it is coupled with doctors' innate reluctance to assist in dying,
would obviously need to build in safeguards which would ensure, so
far as possible, that requests were competent, comprehended and as
free from duress as any choice ever is. So, although these concerns
need to be addressed, they do not by themselves argue against
legalization.

A further argument commonly used against changing the law is
that it is only the first step onto a 'slippery slope'. In other words, if
you allow A to happen, then B (and perhaps even C) will logically
follow. We might approve of A, but B and C are bad consequences and
so A should not be allowed so that B and C don't happen. This
approach also assumes that B and C will never happen if A doesn't.

This is a widely used argument, but one which is in fact rather
weak. Although it could be argued that the removal of prohibitions on
assisting death could lead to an increased tolerance of aid in dying,
this is only a bad consequence if aid in dying is itself wrong.
Moreover, as Beauchamp and Childress[38] point out, 'If dire
consequences will in fact flow from the legal legitimation of assisted
suicide or voluntary active euthanasia, then the argument is cogent,
and such practices are justifiably prohibited. But how good', they ask,
'is the evidence that dire consequences will occur. Does the evidence
indicate that we cannot maintain firm distinctions in public policies

between patient-requested death and involuntary euthanasia?'[39] Their answer is that there is 'scant'[40] evidence to support this view.

Others however, like Giesen,[41] are less sure. He argues that 'Recent history shows us that once firm constraints against killing are removed, a general moral decline will result.'[42] What Giesen has in mind is the Holocaust, but using this as an example is misleading. The genocide which resulted from Nazi policies was not the result of the weakening of individual attitudes to voluntary assistance in dying, nor did it follow from respecting competent decisions. Rather it was an overt, deliberate and calculated policy which **ignored** the wishes of those concerned, driven by the politics of hatred and based on fallacious and degrading assumptions. It has no parallel with respecting the free decisions of individuals.

Even without using the Nazi experience as an example, there are some for whom the slippery slope of argument works. The fear is that legalizing assistance in dying on a voluntary basis would inevitably lead to it being accepted in non-voluntary or involuntary situations. The argument is that if it is in the interests of one person suffering from a particular condition to die, then it must be in the interests of everyone else in the same condition, whether or not they actually ask for it. But this is illogical in the extreme. Death is only deemed to be in the interests of the individual because that is how he or she **personally** sees it – not the relatives, not the doctor, not the state, not any third party. The interest that is being served is not death but autonomy, even though the outcome of the autonomous behaviour is death.

Still others fear that legalizing aid in dying would result in irrevocable damage to the doctor/patient relationship. The patient, it is argued, would fear the doctor who is allowed to assist in dying. But the patient has no need to fear the doctor who is only permitted to help on strictly controlled, transparent and accountable grounds, and most significantly, only on a competent request. Indeed, the patient may have more reason to fear where there are **no** legal controls. Our survey, and others, have shown that – no matter what the law says – doctors are already helping their patients to die without being accountable to anyone and without having their decisions scrutinized (*see Chapter* 5). This surely is much more a legitimate source of concern.

In any event, patients' trust in doctors is not solely dependent on the doctor's capacity to cure, it is also fundamentally rooted in respect. The patient generally respects the doctor, but can reasonably also expect to be respected in return. That respect can be shown by accepting and acting upon the patient's choice. However, physicians may feel uncomfortable with participation in assisted death. Many will appeal to the prohibition in the Hippocratic Oath on bringing about the death of a patient (of which more later). However, as Weir[43] points out, the achievement of other legitimate medical goals, such as alleviating suffering and respect for patients, is every bit as important as 'a literal adherence to an ancient oath whose religious and moral framework is of such limited relevance to contemporary medicine that the Oath is frequently altered when used in medical convocations and increasingly replaced entirely by other kinds of oaths, including those written by medical students themselves.'[44]

It can be concluded, therefore, that there are cogent reasons to be concerned about clinicians assisting in the death of their patients, but ultimately they are arguable. Some are based on grounds which are inherently weak when exposed to cool and critical analysis, others stem from intuition rather than argument. This does not lay claim, however, to throwing caution to the wind. CeloCruz warns against too easily turning physician assisted suicide and euthanasia '... into social practices, institutionalizing and memorializing them.'[45] Caution is appropriate, but it does not mandate failure to shape a law which reflects contemporary morality.

WHY NOT ASSISTED SUICIDE?

Changing the law requires that the concerns expressed above are taken account of, and it is accepted that 'No set of regulations can be perfect.'[46] However, as Dworkin points out, 'it would be perverse to force competent people to die in great pain or in a drugged stupor for that reason, accepting a great and known evil to avoid the risk of a speculative one.'[47]

Claiming the Right
to Aid in Dying

He has lived well who has been able to die
when he has desired to die
Pubillius Syrus

The recognition that medicine cannot guarantee immortality, and that some of its 'cures' or palliations are worse than the underlying disease, has seen an exponential growth in arguments in favour of the 'right' to choose when to die. Equally, a public increasingly concerned to explore and assert its control is questioning more and more why control in life should not include control in death. As Rachels says, 'there are signs that our society is moving away from a rigid insistence that one may never choose the time of one's death.'[1]

From birth to adulthood, the law is increasingly prepared to concede that life is not always preferable to death or non-existence. The move away from strict adherence to the sanctity of all life, witnessed by liberalized abortion laws, judicial tolerance of selective non-treatment of handicapped infants, the incorporation into law of the principle of double effect and the adult's right to refuse life-sustaining treatment, shows that attitudes to death have significantly changed. The paradox, however, is that, apart from in the last of these, we seem to be prepared for third parties to make the decision and not the person directly concerned. In other words, someone else may choose my death for me, but unless I suffer from a particular kind of condition, I may not choose it for myself.

Even those who would argue against legalizing assisted death must see what a fundamentally bizarre situation this is. And it is particularly strange when considering that in the only situation where the request of the patient is allowed to be followed, the reason is substantially grounded in respect for autonomy. What could be more autonomous than a competent request for assistance, and what more disingenuous than to ignore autonomy simply because of the **nature** of the individual's clinical condition? What this means is that, if the condition which I find intolerable is one which needs treatment, I can refuse it and achieve the death of my choosing, but if it is not, and even if my suffering is as great and my desire for death is as strong, my request if acted upon would be tainted with criminality.

Leaving aside for the moment the involvement of third parties which would be necessary in the latter case, especially since it has already been argued that failure to treat renders third parties every bit as complicit in the death, it is worth looking at what must be the strongest argument in favour of assisted death – namely, that it respects the autonomous wishes of a competent person. Although Beauchamp and Childress[2] recognize that autonomy is a difficult concept, none the less they suggest that 'Virtually all theories of autonomy agree that two conditions are essential: 1. *liberty* (independence from controlling influences) and 2. *agency* (capacity for intentional actions).'[3]

Since the latter, which we have broadly described as competence, has already been discussed, we will concentrate here on the former.

Liberty is not simply about being free from outside influences. It also includes the ability genuinely to make a free decision, and this entails the adequate provision of relevant information. To some extent, then, the ability to act autonomously requires a shift in the doctor/patient relationship. As Katz[4] points out: 'It cannot be accidental that the principles of medical ethics have never commanded physicians and their patients to get to know one another so that they can make decisions jointly. We need to enquire why physicians have been so insistent in their demand that all authority be vested in one party – the doctor.'[5]

Clearly, were this tradition to continue it would represent a serious barrier to the truly autonomous choice of patients. To this extent, therefore, the argument for assisted suicide, based on autonomy, is yet one further argument for a change in the power structure of medicine. That doctors are increasingly in favour of the legalization of assisted suicide (see Chapter 5) might equally suggest that this change is already happening. Ideally, then, the patient making a decision that life is no longer the most desirable option should have adequate information about alternatives, but, as Kennedy says, 'It may happen sometimes that the patient may wish to end his life, rather than wait for death.'[6]

As has been suggested, patients who make choices about refusing treatment which could save their lives are making a choice for death which is endorsed by our law, no matter the basis on which it is made. The arguments in favour of assisted death depend critically on the same values which underpin legal acceptance of these decisions. In the Canadian case of Malette v. Shulman[7], for example, a doctor who ignored a card carried by a Jehovah's Witness which indicated that she would refuse blood transfusion was found to have assaulted her even although his actions saved her life. In the US case of Elizabeth Bouvia[8], the patient's right to choose to refuse treatment which was life preserving was upheld, as it was in the English case of Re C.[9].

Since the acts/omissions doctrine is inapplicable in these cases, it is clear that autonomy is what prevails over the preservation of all life. As Brock puts it: 'The judgement of a person who competently decides to commit suicide is essentially that "my expected future life, under the best conditions possible for me, is so bad that I judge it to be worse than no further continued life at all." This seems to be in essence exactly the same judgement that some persons who decide to forego life sustaining treatment make.'[10]

If it is accepted, then, that in reality as well as in rhetoric the choices are no different, then the source of the acceptance of one and the prohibition on the other is elusive at best. It has already been suggested that it might be found in the nature of the patient's condition – that is, in the clinical diagnosis – but this is no moral or ethical basis from which to proceed. It also, of course, hinges on context. Many people will die in institutions, prevented from killing themselves by the regimes which are (rightly) set up to avoid accident or ill-considered actions. But they also prevent, by careful monitoring, the competent person from killing him- or herself, leaving that person dependent on others for the achievement of his or her goal. As Weir says: 'If personal control over one's living and dying is highly valued by the patient, the decisions made about healthcare will reflect that value. In extreme cases, the desire to remain autonomous and in control sometimes includes the request for help from a physician – a request for help in exercising control over one's final exit.'[11]

In other words, the individual may remain competent and autonomous when the decision in favour of death is made, but lack other – physical or contextual – elements essential to the completion of an autonomous act. In these circumstances, the person needs help to ensure that his or her competent choice can be given effect. Generally, this help will come from healthcare workers, most notably doctors, and their role in this will be dealt with later (*see Chapter* 4). For the moment, though, Brandt's [12] comment is of interest. He contends that 'As soon as it is clear beyond reasonable doubt not only that death is now preferable to life, but also that it will be every day from now until the end, the rational thing is to act promptly.'[13] For those who cannot act, the rational thing is to seek help. Beauchamp and Childress point out that if individuals '... have a legal and moral right to refuse treatment that involves healthcare professionals in implementing their decision and bringing about their deaths, we have a reason to suppose they have a similar right to request assistance of willing physicians to help them control the conditions under which they die.'[14]

Put another way, physicians who respect the autonomous refusal of treatment which could save life are already participating in a form of assisted death. They may find it frustrating to watch a patient die who could be saved, but they do not and should not intervene. Nor, apparently, do they see this as a direct infringement of their commitments under professional ethics and codes. The appeal to professional codes, such as the Hippocratic Oath, is a common one when doctors seek to avoid implementing aid in dying, although, as will be seen (Chapter 3), it is one which is undoubtedly open to serious challenge. But in any event, as Brandt has said, 'On this matter a patient's physician has a special obligation, from which any talk about the Hippocratic Oath does not absolve him.'[15]

This 'special obligation' includes both respect for autonomy and a concept much more familiar to medical language – the relief of suffering. Patient-made choices are increasingly encouraged in all aspects of healthcare and – in the absence of compelling arguments that life must always be preferred to death – this is no less true in end-of-life decisions. Patients in this situation should be equally encouraged to demand all relevant information about the nature and consequences of their condition, and equally empowered to decide what to do about it. As has been said, 'What the patient ought not to do is to allow him or herself to succumb to a system in which all the morally relevant choices will be made for him or her ...'[16] Rather, '... the patient must take whatever steps are necessary to ensure that when the time comes, the physician or other decision maker, professional or lay, *will follow his or her desires, not act in his or her interests* – that is, respect the principle of autonomy and not that of beneficence ...'[17]

Yet this is precisely what does not happen and what is not allowed by law. In the scale of values, autonomy is clearly of greater moral worth than is the professionally constructed commitment to beneficence or non-maleficence, yet the latter is given more weight than the former. And, of course, it must be said that it is a particular interpretation of the latter which is used to trump autonomy, dependent entirely on the interpretation of 'good' and 'harm'. It cannot be simplistically assumed that doing good (beneficence) means forcing people to live beyond the point at which it is tolerable for them, nor can it be assumed that avoiding harm (non-maleficence) is constituted by ignoring the suffering of patients and disrespecting their autonomy, yet this is precisely the culture in which healthcare professionals have been steeped.

One example will serve to highlight the possibility that these interpretations need closer scrutiny. Sue Rodriguez[18] was a young Canadian woman suffering from amyotropic lateral sclerosis, a condition which involves deterioration in the capacity to control all basic functions but which can leave the intellect intact. As a mother of young children, and with no certainty as to when she would reach the final, degrading stages of her illness, Ms Rodriguez wished to live for as long as she could cope with her condition. The option of an early suicide would have deprived her of time to enjoy her remaining life and her children.

Under the Canadian Charter of Rights and Freedoms she sought court authority to claim the right to assisted suicide when her own situation became intolerable. Although her plight inevitably aroused great sympathy, the court refused (by a narrow majority) to interpret the Charter as giving her such a right. Her ultimate achievement of a dignified death in her own time and after making a competent decision was the result of the courage of a physician acting outside of the law. It is not fantasy to speculate that the dignity of her death, and the comfort of its availability, were marred for Ms Rodriguez by the knowledge that those who showed the courage and the compassion to help her were possibly (although, as it turned out, not in fact) to be subjected to severe professional and legal sanction because the law refused her right to choose death in the ghastly circumstances which she endured. The ultimate harm in this situation was not her death but rather that – had she been able to commit suicide or had there been life-saving treatment which she could have refused – she would have been lawfully permitted the option of death, with the same outcome, but with less anxiety and publicity.

Autonomy may be the strongest argument in favour of assisted death, particularly when it is so obvious that it is widely recognized as a fundamental moral value. It is by no means the only argument, however. Closely allied to it is another principle which societies hold dear – namely, that of respect for persons. Although these two principles may overlap, there is a difference which is of particular significance for those whose autonomy is seen to be at risk because of the nature of their physical or emotional condition.

Autonomy is the preserve of those with the capacity to exercise it. Respect, however, is due to all. Thus, for example, no matter what state individuals may be in, the Kantian imperative demands that they are treated as an end in themselves and not as a means to an end. There is an intrinsic value in each person which militates against treating him or her in ways which deny dignity. As Pellegrino has said, 'Human beings, whether as individuals or aggregates, are inherently entitled to respect: they possess an inviolable dignity.'[19] In more legalistic terms, Kennedy puts it this way: 'Perhaps the most fundamental precept of the common law is respect for the liberty of the individual. In a medical-legal context this means that a person's right to self-determination, to deal with his body as he sees fit, is protected by law. The doctor's first duty is to respect this right. This applies as much to the terminally ill patient as to any other.'[20]

Respect, therefore, is due to the individual's decisions by virtue of his or her **being** an individual. Because in the clinical setting this respect may sometimes be reduced by an apparent lack of autonomy, it can sometimes be the case that respect is directly (although perhaps inadvertently) challenged because of the physical or psychological condition of the person. But clinical condition is irrelevant to the respect which is due, and in this sense it is a greater value than that of autonomy, and provides a further ethical basis from which to conclude that it is **failure** to carry out the request of the patient which should be the exception rather than the norm.

Respect in such circumstances can be shown in a number of ways. It may be shown by the mere fact of caring, by the provision of optimal and maximal palliation and emotional support, but it may also be shown by ending suffering by permitting or assisting death. In fact, this already happens, not just in a passive way, but also in an active one. When doctors use the principle of double effect to increase analgaesia in the knowledge that this may hasten death but not (or at least so it is alleged) with the intention that death will result, they are actively bringing about a foreseen and foreseeable death (with or without the patient's agreement). Since intention cannot be proved, in what way does this differ from helping the patient who wants to die? In reality, the only difference is that in the latter the patient is the instigator, a fact which makes it more rather than less morally satisfactory. Autonomy-based arguments ask much of the individual making the decision; respect asks much of the person with the capacity to implement it.

Respect also involves doing unto others as you would wish to be done to. Yet in a survey of her colleagues at the University of Chicago

Hospital, one doctor found that, although opposing the legalization of assisted suicide, they indicated that they would use the means to which they had access to end their own lives when they decided that would be appropriate.[21] In other words, the doctors who have the means to act autonomously and without third-party assistance concede that life in some circumstances would be intolerable for them but refuse to respect the same decision on the part of a patient. They would avail themselves of an option which their patients do not have, and which apparently they do not wish their patients to have. Whatever the motivation for this, it recognizes neither autonomy nor respect.

Battin[22] argues that the individual should not be made 'a "patient" in not only a medical but a moral sense ...',[23] and concludes that 'Among the indignities that medicine is capable of inflicting, this may be among the most profound.'[24] Respect for the person, then, may mean accepting that statements made about life and death should be viewed as *prima facie* valid, with compelling evidence needed to show why they should **not** be so treated. Respect for persons requires respect for their decisions whether or not we are comfortable with them, but the tradition of physicians and the law has been to err on the side of paternalism – effectively to err in favour of life, even when it is unwanted. Of course, as has been pointed out, '... the law must protect people who think it would be appalling to be killed, even if they had only painful minutes to live. But the law must also protect those with the opposite conviction: that it would be appalling not to be offered an easier, calmer death with the help of doctors they trust. Making a person die in a way that others approve, but that affronts his own dignity, is a serious, unnecessary form of tyranny.'[25]

A combination of autonomy and respect makes for a convincing and powerful set of arguments in favour of permitting people to choose their own death. Moreover, these principles are superior, and not subjugated, to any professional commitment held by third parties. To be sure, no one should be forced to participate in an assisted death, since they too are entitled to act autonomously and to be treated with respect. As Weir says, 'Physician assisted suicide should be motivated by compassion for a patient, not a misplaced sense of moral obligation.'[26]

There are further arguments which support the case for physician assisted suicide, not least that which stems from the alleviation of suffering. The person who concludes that life is no longer worth living is someone whose particular suffering has reached the point of being unbearable. And again it is worth remembering that suffering is a wider concept than pain. As Callahan says, 'Pain may be described as a distressing, hurtful sensation in the body. Suffering, by contrast, is a broader, more complex idea. Each may be defined, in the case of illness, as a sense of anguish, vulnerability, loss of control and threat to the integrity of the self. There can be pain without suffering and suffering without pain.'[30]

Although by and large we have no obligation to alleviate the suffering of others or even to prevent it happening, most people would intuitively see this as a good thing. For doctors there is an additional reason for this – namely, the nature of their business. The doctor's task is intimately linked with the relief of suffering, a concept which is wider than that of cure. Since, 'Healing, like any other activity, brings with it limits ...',[28] it is important that clinicians are as alert to the responsibilities that go with alleviation of suffering as they are to those which surround cure.

Yet, despite this, there are some who would stop short of alleviating suffering when the only way of achieving it is to help someone to die. This is, of course, a matter of individual conscience, quite apart from the legal position, but it can none the less be unravelled without threatening individual morality. As has already been seen, the form of alleviation may in fact be precisely what the doctor would want to achieve for him- or herself – relief from situations such as '... indignity, confusion, disorientation, sedation, the need for constant care, boredom, loneliness, lying in your own excrement, inability to function on any level that allows enjoyment, simple emotional anguish, fear ...'[29] What humanity can be said to be achieved by allowing 'professional guidelines' to prevent the alleviation of such horrors? When the very real and humane desire to rescue individuals from such suffering is coupled with the competent request of the sufferer in such a situation, there would have to be very firm evidence indeed which would morally support a failure to act upon the person's wish for alleviation, even if that act resulted in his or her death.

There are further, although for some less appealing, arguments which support a change in the law. One classic argument would be from the perspective of the utilitarian. Utilitarian arguments are sometimes unpopular because for many they are the direct antithesis of arguments based on human rights, which have become the most popular and powerful arguments of this century. Yet, in addition to the rights-based arguments already explored, utilitarian arguments can also be used to support assisted suicide. The fathers of utilitarianism – Jeremy Bentham and John Stuart Mill – may approach their philosophy from slightly different perspectives, but the views of each can be called in aid of the argument presented here.

For Bentham, '... the essence of morality is not the service of God, or obedience to abstract rules, but the promotion of the greatest possible happiness for creatures on earth.'[30] Mill argued that the only justification for intervening in the actions of an individual was when these actions had a negative effect on others. Each formulation emphasizes – one in a positive and one in a negative way – the cumulative effect of individual decisions as being the critical test of moral validity. Thus, if permitting certain behaviour diminishes collective 'happiness' or intrudes on the rights of others, it is immoral.

Donne said, 'Any man's death diminishes me'.[31] This might be taken to imply that all steps should be taken to postpone death since it does not contribute to the maximization of happiness. However, such an interpretation is manifest nonsense. Every person must die and some decisions for death are already allowed without a noticeably deleterious effect on the community. The real question is whether or not allowing people to have active assistance in their death would fall foul of the utilitarian credo which favours addressing the consequences of permitted actions. It must be conceded that this is not a question which can be answered by reference to direct empirical evidence, but to the kind of analysis already undertaken of situations where death is assisted, albeit passively.

Whatever our concerns about the way in which we deal with handicapped infants, patients in persistent vegetative state and so on, there is no evidence that legal endorsement of that treatment has brought society to its knees. Nor is there evidence which suggests that the doctors who support and participate in such decisions have suddenly lost all moral sense and have systematically set about killing other patients. Indeed, what can be said is that these decisions have generally been reached with the agreement, or on the initiative, of doctors and relatives. That the death of the person affects them is not in doubt – that it would affect them if it happened naturally is also true. But their support for these decisions could be said to have increased rather than reduced happiness.

It is plausible, therefore, that utilitarian arguments would also support assistance in dying. Doctors may prolong unwanted life for a number of reasons – misguided beneficence, cultural credo or fear of prosecution. But for those for whom the thought of being kept alive against their wishes is untenable the sum of happiness is undoubtedly reduced and the result is an indictment on the system. As Rachels argues, 'There are times when the protection of human life has no point, and the western tradition has had difficulty acknowledging this. The noble ideal of "protecting human life" is invoked even when the life involved does the subject no good and even when it is not wanted.'[32] In both human rights and utilitarian terms, refusal to recognize this must contribute significantly to the moral tone of the community – in other words, it both minimizes happiness and denies autonomy.

One highly controversial argument in favour of allowing assisted death concerns the use of scarce resources. No amount of rhetorical prohibition on considering resources can disguise the fact that this is a real and important concern of modern healthcare. No matter how great the investment in healthcare (estimated, for example, to be about 15 per cent of the gross domestic product in the US[33]), supply will never meet demand. Using these resources to keep someone alive who wishes to die could be seen as irresponsible and also as conflicting with the interests of others who may be denied treatment as a result.

It is, of course, morally difficult to swallow the notion that resources should predict life or death, but this is not what this argument seeks to do. Rather, it adds one further piece of weight to the view that neither individuals nor communities would necessarily be harmed by permitting competent decisions to be vindicated. However, there is one concern which does relate to resources and which must be addressed. Given that people may reach a decision for death because they feel themselves to be a burden, might the fact that they know themselves to be using up resources which could help others not be an additional source of duress and an additional reason to doubt that their decision really is a free one?

The answer is that it may indeed be a factor in a decision, but this need not necessarily be a bad thing. Indeed, it could also be a factor in the decision of those who are allowed to refuse life-saving treatment, although it is not in that case taken to be a reason to force treatment upon them. A decision based on altruism is not one which is inherently based on duress. Battin points out that 'Particularly significant and problematic are the altruistic choices a severely ill or dying patient may make. His non-medical decision can range over all the aspects of his life over which he retains control – for instance, the disposition of his property, the bestowing of affection or advice, the assertion of his political power or cultural influence, and so forth ...'[34] Yet, as she concludes, '... the institution of medicine appears to respect overt expression of it only in quite restricted forms.'[35] So too, in prohibiting assisted suicide, does the law.

Yet failure to respect altruistic motives, as well as those which might be described as more selfish – for example the relief of suffering – denies the individual death on his or her own terms and for reasons which he or she respects. As Kass has pointed out: 'Even the *ordinary* methods of treating disease and prolonging life have changed the context in which men die. Fewer and fewer people die in the familiar surroundings of home or in the company of family and friends. At that time of life when there is perhaps the greatest need for human warmth and comfort, the dying patient is kept company by cardiac pacemakers and defibrillators, respirators, aspirators, oxygenators, catheters and his intravenous drip. Ties to the community of man are replaced by attachments to an assemblage of machines.'[36] The desire to build altruism into the other facets of the decision to die is one which may help to re-establish ties to the 'community of man'. It may be a positive and affirming part of the difficult process which the individual is undergoing.

Finally, it could be argued that since assisted death is happening anyway, we should act to rationalize it within the legal and moral framework. The *Boston Globe*, for example, reported in 1992 that 'one in five US physicians say they have deliberately taken action to cause a patient's death ... Almost one-fourth of the internal specialists said a terminally ill patient had asked them for assistance in committing suicide.'[37] Although our survey results showed considerably lower figures than these (*see Chapter* 5), they endorse the view that physicians already do defy the law to help patients to die. However, generally speaking this is an intellectually unconvincing argument. Murder, rape and theft happen too, but our response is not to say, 'In that case they should be legalized.' More than mere occurrence would be needed if this argument were to hold any water at all.

Some support may be derived from public attitudes. In our survey, 67 per cent of the population were in favour of a change in the law to permit assistance in dying; 54 per cent of doctors and pharmacists were also in favour (*see Chapter 5*). Harris Poll No. 9 (1995), released on 30th January 1995, surveyed 1,250 adults in the US, following the immense publicity surrounding Dr Jack Kevorkian's use of his 'suicide machine'. Of the sample interviewed, 94 per cent had heard of Dr Kevorkian; his behaviour was approved of by 58 per cent of that group, with 39 per cent disapproving. By 70 per cent to 27 per cent the doctors believed that the law should 'allow doctors to comply with the wishes of a dying patient in severe distress who asks to have his or her life ended'. And 67 per cent said they would approve of a law such as that passed in Oregon which would legalize physician assisted suicide in certain prescribed situations.

There are many more surveys, and what emerges from all of them is that the tide is shifting in favour of a managed death. It must be repeated that this is at best anecdotal evidence, but the fact that it is relatively constant no matter where it is discovered and no matter how often the question is asked might be thought to elevate it slightly above mere anecdote. Of course, public and medical opinion are no reasons to change the law if we believe that assistance in death is always wrong and we can produce coherent reasons for holding such a position. But, in fact, what has gone before shows that we do not always believe this, that we are merely picky about the way in which death is contrived. Philosophically, Beauchamp and Childress propose that the rightness or wrongness of an act depends 'on the merit of the justification underlying the action, not the type of action it is.

Neither killing nor letting die, therefore, is per se wrongful, and in this regard they are to be distinguished from murder, which is per se wrongful. Both killing and letting die are prima facie wrong, but can be justified under some circumstances.'[38]

If this assertion is accepted, and it is agreed that the relief of suffering following a competent request is a justification for viewing assistance in dying as a good thing, then the fact that it is already happening with no obvious adverse effects might make for one small step along the path to legalization. In addition, the fact that it is already happening, if taken even marginally seriously, points to one further matter of considerable importance.

If it is not wrong to help competent patients to die, it can become wrong if it is not done in the appropriate circumstances and within agreed guidelines. For those currently doing it, there is no such scrutiny. Decisions will be made on personal bases, with no accountability (unless the law becomes involved) and with no transparency. That this is unsatisfactory is without doubt. As Shavelson points out: 'The present prohibition against legal assistance in suicide has guaranteed that not a single physician has ever assisted in the death of a patient while following set rules, nor under the observation of her peers, nor under the watchful eyes of the law. Yet surveys of doctors have found that up to 37 per cent have, in secrecy, aided in the death of a terminally ill patient. While the public expresses fear of abuse of assisted suicide, no one is overseeing those physicians who have already made aid in suicide part of their medical practice.'[39]

It can be seen, therefore, that there are strong reasons for legalizing physician assisted suicide – arguments which trump those against. Most significantly, helping people at this most critical time in their lives is offering them respect. As Quill, *et al.* say 'it is not idiosyncratic, selfish or indicative of a psychiatric disorder for people with an incurable illness to want some control over how they die. The

idea of a noble, dignified death, with a meaning that is deeply
personal and unique is exalted in great literature, poetry, art, and
music.'[40] It is also something about which increasing numbers of
people care. Even if very few ever took advantage of the legal
availability of assisted suicide, the mere fact that it was possible
might provide comfort and reassurance.

It is often said that consensual medicine, based on mutual trust,
is the best medicine. For the moment, patients cannot trust that their
doctor will help them out in their moments of deepest suffering, and
equally – because of the shadowy world in which those physicians
who are prepared to help must exist – patients also do not know
whether or not decisions will be made in which they have no role.
The sick, the elderly, the suffering will continue to fear either being
inappropriately allowed to die or inappropriately kept alive, unless
clarity replaces obfuscation. As Weir says: 'PAS seems to be both
necessary and morally justifiable in rare cases and, if handled
correctly by morally responsible physicians, need not threaten the
foundation of trust that is critical to patient-physician relationships.'[41]
Even more importantly, it will allow people to come to their death
empowered, not disenfranchised – controlled, not helpless.

Hippocrates and Medical Ethics

Thou alone, O Death, art the healer of deadly ills
Aeschylus

Medical ethics have played a significant role in shaping societies' response to suffering, healing and the choice for life or death. In particular, one of the earliest attempts to construct an ethical code, the Hippocratic Oath, continues to be used as one of the main reasons given as to why doctors should not assist a patient to die. On the other hand, critics of the Hippocratic Oath point to its inability to serve any useful purpose in contemporary medical practice.[1] Since appeal to Hippocrates is so common an argument against the involvement of doctors in assisting death, before considering why doctors should be the authorized third parties in assisted suicide it is necessary to analyse in some depth whether or not the appeal to Hippocratic tradition can provide a compelling argument against physician assisted suicide.

The evolution of medical ethics cannot be viewed as a neatly packaged set of principles. Instead their development has been protracted and piecemeal, reflecting the morality and influences of the particular period of time in which they arose. In other words, ethics need time to develop, they need to be thought about, written down and debated,[2] but more importantly, the time involved in their development shows that they are not cast in stone; that to survive they need flexibility.

Like other codes, the Hippocratic corpus developed over time, but much of what is appealed to today is one small part of it, the Oath, parts of which suffer from having been given the status of a timeless truth. Rather than acknowledging its limitations – the constraints of the time and the expertise available – the Oath has become for some the ultimate statement of truth rather than it being accepted, as Clements has said, that 'The history of medical ethics parallels the history of philosophical ethics, and at its best is an honest attempt to determine what the right thing to do is in the practice of medicine.'[3]

Throughout the centuries, medicine has been practised with an air of mystery surrounding it. The assumption was that some special understanding was required to practise medicine. Therefore its practice was limited to groups of people to whom this knowledge was passed down from generation to generation, or to those who were educated in the formal sense. In other words, its development was sufficiently institutionalized to allow information and knowledge to be passed on. Influenced by culture and time, throughout history different groups of people have been seen as having this special knowledge. Healing could come in many forms and from different sources, for example witch doctors, who often relied on basic superstition; priests, who employed an arguably more developed superstition in the form of religion; and philosophers, whose medical practice often reflected quite sophisticated philosophic reasoning. At various times, these groups were all seen as purveyors of medicine.

The influences of these three main groups varied. Witch doctors, for example, were often called to ward off evil spirits or encourage good ones. 'Cures' for inclement weather or a potion to ensure victory in combat would also be within their ambit. The powerful influence of religion meant that illness could also be construed as a punishment from God for committing a 'sin'. Priests, already enjoying great reverence and status, were turned to for a 'cure' and perceived as having a supernatural medical ability.

Even today, when faced with ill-health or awareness of mortality, many people turn to their God or his representatives for help in either this life or the next. However, in contemporary Western societies, the person to whom the individual will most likely look for healing or reassurance in ill-health will be the doctor, in conjunction with, or without, God. The expansion of the role of the doctor and of orthodox medicine may be seen as a kind of contemporary parallel of the historical gaining of power and authority of religion and its priests.

Hellenic medicine took a completely different approach. Whereas magic and priestly practices were primarily based on instinct and observations of nature, Hellenic medicine was developed within the framework of the Greek philosophic schools. Instinct still prevailed but it was coupled with scientific enquiry, observation, discussion and analysis.

But all of this requires a framework. No matter the form that the practice of a profession takes, it is generally guided by some ethical constraints. In medicine, this has taken the form of the Hippocratic Oath, which gives certainty to the doctor seeking reassurance about his or her professionalism. As Richter says, 'To make people believe in something makes them ten times more powerful.'[4]

Unlike many other forms of regulations and rules, an oath can be seen as a very individual and personal thing. It is possible to be unaware of or to disregard many regulations, but one actually 'takes' an oath. Therefore it would be difficult to deny knowledge of its contents once it has been taken. An oath, therefore, has undeniable symbolism in developing a professional ethic. Adhering to its provisions may create a sense of unity, it may reassure the individual that a benchmark exists. It can also unify groups and raise their prestige in society. Richter claims its importance is even more pervasive, suggesting that 'An oath is a sort of handshake in a network, which is the structure for future society.'[5]

It is by no means clear when the Hippocratic Oath was composed, but it would not be unreasonable to suggest that it evolved at a time when the priests in Greek medicine temples were losing their position of authority over their patients. People were questioning their supposed expertise, and certainly it would be wrong to assume that early Greek medicine had any great sophistication. The practice of medicine in ancient Greece was diverse; expertise varied both in breadth and depth. The physician could be a trained master craftsman or simply a novice.[6] Homer provides a good account of ancient Greek medical practices, and the *Iliad* highlights the fact that religion and magic were still influential[7], so there were plenty of charlatans offering magical cures and potions. Many felt that they had medical knowledge, at least to a certain extent, and were willing to use it. Greek medicine was therefore a relatively uncertain affair, the practitioners' competence could have been limited, their methods were varied and practices unregulated. So, around 400 BC, the time was right for an extended family of about seven doctors to transform medicine into a 'modern science', and the family name of Hippocrates became one of the most famous in history.[8]

The Hippocrates we tend to associate with the Oath was born on the Greek island of Kos around 460 BC. He was the second in the line of seven doctors and was apparently small, ugly and bald, with a big nose.[9] What he lacked in stature, he made up for in bravery, going to Athens during the plague in 430 BC. Like many of the early physicians, it is thought that Hippocrates travelled widely. He died in Thessalia in 377 BC.[10]

Research has shown that the famous Oath which is attributed to Hippocrates was not in fact solely his work but encompassed a wide range of doctrines, styles and ideas, written by many individuals over at least 150 years.[11] However, although the Hippocratic school became the most well known, it was certainly not the only one. Large schools developed in a Greek settlement in Asia Minor and on the island of Sicily, and there is evidence of smaller schools in Rhodes and Cyrene.[12]

It seems likely that Hippocrates contributed four books to the 'Corpus Hippocraticum', which comprises about 70 such books. The book of *Epidemics* provides descriptions of typhus and diphtheria, and of his first-hand evidence of the plague. Hippocrates also wrote about epilepsy and the relationship between environment and health.[13]

The Hippocratic corpus as a whole describes the Hippocratean traditions and was probably one of the first attempts to lay down principles of medical ethics. It is interesting that out of the 70 books that were written, the Oath is the best known and most enduring part of the work.

Hippocrates' philosophy of his daily experiences of life are contained in the book of *Aphorisms*. The first aphorism and perhaps the best known notes that 'The life is so short, the art so long to learn, the chance soon gone, experience deceptive and judgement difficult.'[14] In many ways, it might be thought that this sentiment is infinitely more timeless than the content of the Oath itself, which will be discussed below.

In 1943, Ludwig Edelstein carried out a detailed analysis of the Hippocratic Oath and concluded that it was heavily influenced by the Pythagorean school of philosophy. The writings and the perceptions of the Pythagorean school are important on two counts. First, the way in which they viewed illness and disease was very influential on the contents of the Oath. For example, all the writings were based on the notion that the universe was made up of four basic elements: wetness, dryness, warmth and cold. Furthermore, the Greeks thought that

humankind was a replica of the universe, so logically these basic
elements would be replicated within the human body. They were
represented by fluids or 'humours', namely blood, phlegm, yellow bile
and black bile. An equal proportion of these four humours would
ensure good health; excesses either way would result in a recognizable
disease.[15] Secondly, it is worth noting that despite the profound effect
that the Oath has had on medical practice and ethics, the Pythagorean
school represented only a small minority of Greek philosophical
opinion.

That the Hippocratic school shifted the balance from the strong
influences of the priests to the more structured and reasoned
influences of the Greek philosophers can be demonstrated in the
following three ways. First, the Hippocratic physician took a realistic
approach as to what could actually be done for a patient. In the early
stages of medical ethics, the concern was that the public was given a
realistic prognosis of what could be done. There is, no doubt, some
self-interest here, as it would not do for the medical profession to be
seen killing off more people than it cured, so explaining limitations in
advance would doubtless keep a check on the expectations of
patients. In contrast, modern society seems to have high expectations
of medicine. Both patients and doctors anticipate that the practice of
medicine will involve some active intervention. There is, however,
nothing in the Hippocratic Oath which promotes such tampering.
Indeed, Hippocrates observed that doctors should do their best not to
kill their patients with treatment and argued that with decent
hygiene and a sensible diet most people get better anyway. As
Gaarder explains, 'The most essential safeguards against sickness,
according to the Hippocratic medical tradition, were moderation and
a healthy lifestyle. When sickness occurs, it is a sign that nature has
gone off course because of physical or mental imbalance.'[16]

This is consistent with the Pythagorean school of philosophy,
which considered that most illness could be attributed to opulent

living. Considering the excessive eating and drinking that many of the wealthy Greeks enjoyed, it is likely that this observation may well have been based on fact. Nor is it incompatible with the 'natural balance' argument of the four basic elements. This approach to dietetics was a critical feature of the original Oath, but is one which appears to have lost favour over the centuries with the advent of technological medicine.

Secondly, and related to the above, the Hippocratic corpus was a 'struggle for respectability'[17] and, as Cowley notes, 'While conscious of his limited capabilities, the Hippocratic physician was undoubtedly committed to the restoration of health and the alleviation of suffering. Beyond such general standards, however, the corpus suggested that the medical community was largely unregulated, and that physician conduct varied widely. The practice of medicine lacked any enforceable rules of conduct.'[18] Thus the primary purposes of the medical ethic during Hippocratic times were to raise the standard of medical practice and to exclude those who used less competent or more dubious methods.

Thirdly, the Hippocratic school debunked the notion that illness was a punishment for sin. Instead, disease was regarded as a natural biological event, and this promoted a more realistic attitude towards illness and death.

In the Middle Ages priestly influence returned, for medicine was unable to quell the rampant spread of plague. The practice of medicine stagnated during this time. However, the seventeenth century witnessed the eclipse of religious domination and the ascendancy of medical potential. Kafka describes this beautifully: 'That's the way they are, the people in my district. Always asking the impossible of their doctor. They have lost the old faith; the priest sits at home and picks the vestments to pieces one by one; but the doctor, with his sensitive surgical hand, is expected to do everything.'[19]

Thereafter, a further development occurs. In an attempt to reconcile the new thinking with the old, religious influences and

Hippocratic traditions seemed to merge. This is not surprising, for if we accept that the writers of the Oath were from the Pythagorean school, their piety was very compatible with Christian teachings, for example the contents of the Ten Commandments. The overall result was a strict adherence to the principles of the Hippocratic Oath, in particular to those concerning the sanctity of life, but without the realism that accompanied the original thoughts and writings. Cowley *et al.* sum up this period: 'Moral theologians gave considerable attention to the ascendance of the medical profession, and continued to extol the sanctity of life. Within the medical community, the codified and christianised ethical principles of Hippocrates were firmly established and religiously followed.'[20]

Once established, these principles of medical ethics were consolidated and survived successfully and relatively unquestioned until the mid-twentieth century. However, it is suggested that medical developments within the past 50 years have presented the most serious challenge yet to the Hippocratic Oath.

There are many theories as to why this has occurred. What does seem clear is that, as more choices in people's lives have become available, individuals have wished to have a more active say in the making of these choices rather than leaving decisions to be made by others. Medical decisions are perhaps but one example of this. A further milestone was the legal recognition of values such as autonomy, as evidenced by the early twentieth-century decision in *Schloendorff v. Society of New York Hospital*,[21] which led to the development of doctrines such as informed consent. Once rooted within the public consciousness, discussions of these principles and doctrines became more intense.

The changes cannot, however, be solely attributed to legal developments, and it is possible to identify other factors which have changed the fabric of society. The twentieth century has witnessed radical political and social change. Two World Wars have had a profound effect on people's lives, bringing with them as they did rapid advances in technology. Medical technology was no exception, but knowledge that can be used can also be abused, and the legacy of the 'eugenics' policies of Hitler is still one of the main arguments used against legalizing medical assistance to end life. There is, however, no empirical evidence which would allow a conclusion as to which of these forces proved to be the most significant in modifying society's ethical codes.

There can, however, be no doubt that medical advances changed the approach of both individuals and doctors to the practice of medicine, while seeming to leave the Hippocratic Oath relatively unscathed. Doctors still took the Oath (or a modern equivalent) on graduation, and turned to its terms for resolution of ethical dilemmas and as a foundation of 'good' practice. But much had changed.

Advances in medicine shifted the focus from survival to issues of prevention and quality of life. Social and political change generated different expectations of life itself and of medicine. The ethos of medicine was, unsurprisingly, affected by its new capacities. Progress removed constraints, with advances in microscopy, anaesthesia and microbiology being particularly important.

These developments served to overcome the age-old problems of sanitation and sepsis. Freed from these threats to health and well-being, survival was not the struggle that it had once been. When combined with the development of immunization, and the isolation of penicillin in 1940, Western civilizations had reached the stage where there was a greater concern about the **quality** of survival than ever before. As Callahan notes, 'the most potent social impact of medical advancement is the way it reshapes our notions of what it is to have a life.'[22] As medicine showed what it could do, the Hippocratic tradition of non-intervention was replaced by a new imperative – to do everything medically possible to increase a person's longevity. Expectations increased and medicine and those who practised it knew no limits. As Callahan notes, 'Medicine and healthcare have ... entered a new stage of their history, one where the successes of medicine and not its failures alas – in the way they interact with our values – have been the main source of our problems. That success has raised expectations beyond a sustainable point, addicted the system to an unending search for new and usually expensive technological solutions (many of them occasioned by earlier technological solutions)...[23]

In transforming the practice of medicine from one of minimalist involvement to one which mandates increased intervention, it is arguable that scientific advances have already reduced the relevance of the Hippocratic Oath. It is indisputable that much of the Hippocratic tradition was founded on what medicine actually could do at that time. Although there are some values expressed in the Oath which may be described as universal, there is a close link between capacity and the guidance given to doctors about what should be done. The Oath was composed in the light of what was socially acceptable and medically possible at the time it was written. Technology and knowledge have advanced since Hippocrates, at some times more rapidly than at others, but these changes have posed a challenge to some of the specific commitments in the Oath. The general commitments of the Oath can be found in most modern statements of medical ethics, but many of its specific provisions have already been overtaken.

Our expectations of what medicine can do not only seem to have increased in depth but also in breadth. For example, over the past 50 years what is regarded as being a matter of 'health' has expanded dramatically. Improved techniques for birth, assistance in procreation, the re-sculpting of our perceived physical imperfections, preventive screening processes and ultimately seeking a perfect or at least a controlled death have all been crammed into the category of healthcare.

This tends to result in more and more aspects of our lives being viewed from a medical perspective, so that when something goes wrong we have become increasingly dependent upon the medical profession to correct it. This in turn can create unrealistic expectations of those who have to try to 'cure' the ever-expanding list of what constitutes a 'medical' condition, and generates an increasing imbalance of power in the relationship between doctor and patient. This in itself does not actually suggest that the Oath cannot be followed either pragmatically or philosophically. However, because the scope of 'health' and the potential of medicine have altered so dramatically, it may provide a reason to address the question of the Oath's contemporary relevance.

None the less, there are clearly some echoes of Hippocrates which continue to reverberate, for example his exhortation 'as to disease, make a habit of two things – to help, or at least to do no harm.'[24]

This guidance has been translated into the current cornerstones of modern medical ethics, namely the principles of beneficence and non-maleficence. Beneficence applies almost exclusively to the doctor's daily professional actions, for example preserving life, restoring health, and the relief of suffering. Non-maleficence refers to its traditional corollary: first do no harm. Beauchamp and Childress suggest that the principle of beneficence potentially demands more than that of non-maleficence, because beneficence involves a positive action to help others. In comparison, the principle of non-maleficence tends to encompass negative prohibitions on action. Thus the positive codes of conduct override the negative ones.[25]

It is these positive perceptions of restoring, preserving and healing that have come under the most scrutiny and, arguably, attack in the last 30 or so years. None the less, contemporary formulations of medical ethics have much in common with the general terms of the Hippocratic Oath. For example, each contains an equivalent to the exhortation to 'do no harm', the obligation of confidentiality, and so on.

However, whilst the general commitments may remain valid there are some specific provisions which may be subject to re-interpretation in the light of changing values and increased knowledge. In what is usually referred to as the ethical section of the Hippocratic Oath, three major 'do nots' have been challenged: first the performing of surgery, second the performing of abortion and third, providing assistance to end life.

Surgery is now a specialist and respected branch of medical practice, yet it was ruled out by the terms of the Hippocratic Oath. There may be a number of reasons for this prohibition, but one very plausible explanation is that, in the absence of modern capacities, surgery was simply too dangerous to contemplate. In other words, the basis for the prohibition was just as likely to be found in pragmatics as in ethics. The fact that modern medicine has chosen to ignore this prohibition lends weight to this suggestion. However, it also lends credibility to the challenge posed in this chapter to the fundamental value of the Oath itself.

Equally, the Oath's prohibition on pregnancy termination may originally have had both a pragmatic and an ethical basis. The ethics, however, have been reassessed over the years so that abortion is now an accepted (if not universally welcomed) aspect of medical practice.[26] Thus, doctors can be seen to have adopted a rather selective interpretation of the Oath. By so doing they are acknowledging that, particularly in its specific provisions, the Oath may have a temporal rather than an eternal validity. However, one final taboo remains, namely the prohibition on assisting in the death of a patient.

There are two parts of the Oath which bear directly on this issue. The first is the general provision to 'at least do no harm' and more specifically to the statement, 'I will neither give a deadly drug to anyone if asked for it, nor will I make a suggestion to this effect.'

With regard to the general provision, Beauchamp and Childress note that the phrase did not in fact originate from the Hippocratic corpus and suggest that the statement 'at least, do no harm' is a 'strained translation of a single Hippocratic passage'.[27] None the less, this is a fundamental tenet of modern medical ethics. Whether or not this provision directly emanates from the Hippocratic Oath, it is one with which most people would find it difficult to argue. As a basis for the good practice of medicine, it is probably generally accepted as being both useful and morally appropriate.

However, merely to accept this statement as a mantra is to ignore the fact that it tells us nothing about what is meant by 'harm'. Even in its more positive rendering – that is as a positive obligation to act beneficently by doing good – there is no definition of what is 'good'. Thus, we may accept the general proposition, but we must analyse it for content and context before it actually constrains or permits certain behaviour.

In any event, the obligations of beneficence and non-maleficence *can* be found in the Hippocratic Oath, for example, 'I will use treatment to help the sick according to my ability and judgement, but I will never use it to injure or wrong them.' There is no evidence, however, in this passage of the Oath to suggest that doctors had to treat their patients and save their lives whatever the consequences. Rather, they were not to injure or wrong them. The Hippocratic writings illustrate the duty of medicine quite clearly:

In general terms it is to do away with the sufferings of the sick, to lessen the violence of their diseases, and to refuse to treat those who are over-mastered by their diseases, realizing that in such cases medicine is powerless.[28]

The emphasis is on not injuring or causing harm. But, as has already been noted, harm is not a rigid concept and what constitutes harm is something which is not solely definable according to what Hippocrates thought. Contemporary patients and society have an interest in contributing to its definition.

With regard to the second, more specific provision, it is well established that Greek and Roman physicians, even those who were Hippocratic, often supplied their patients with the means to commit suicide despite the injunction against assistance in suicide embodied in the Hippocratic Oath. In other words, even in its earliest times, the Oath was not universally adhered to. This doesn't mean that it **should** not have been, but it does suggest that the apparently absolute nature of this provision was not accepted even at the time it was written. Society's broad acceptance of this practice may be evidenced by the fact that suppliers were not only physicians. Others included Athenian magistrates, who kept a supply of hemlock for those who wished to end their own lives.[29] Emile Durkheim cites Libanius:

Whoever no longer wishes to live shall state his reasons to the Senate, and after having received permission shall abandon life. If your existence is hateful to you, die; if you are overwhelmed by fate, drink the hemlock. If you are bowed with grief, abandon life. Let the unhappy man recount his misfortune, let the magistrate supply him with the remedy and his wretchedness will come to an end.[30]

Essentially, however, for the physician in Greek and Roman times, and indeed for many years afterwards, there was one fundamental question – whether or not the patient would live. The practice of assisting in the death of those patients who would not live was the doctor's only 'remedy'. The modern doctor, however, faces a much wider range of options and a much more complex set of ethical considerations.

Modern medicine can keep people alive who would otherwise have died; it can salvage the nearly dead; it can maintain insensate existence; it can alleviate much pain. In other words, the true ethical dilemma for the modern doctor is the extent to which what can be done can blunt the edges of a desire for death, thus rendering a request for assistance in dying less intelligible. In many ways, this may have resulted in the development of practices which are as much based on sophistry as on fundamental principles.

Margaret Battin makes an interesting comparison between the practice at the time of the Oath and current medical attitudes. She notes the Oath's clear prohibition '... of the then current practice among mainstream Greek physicians of providing euthanatic drugs on request to patients they could not cure ...' and compares it with 'The American Medical Association's 1973 policy statement that the physician is always morally prohibited from killing patients but is not morally bound to preserve life in all cases.'[31]

She suggests that this comparison actually shows the same categorical assertion – that is, that even if a physician may sometimes allow a patient to die, the physician must never kill.

However, this assertion rests on the philosophically dubious distinction between acts and omissions, which has also been challenged both philosophically and in some recent legal decisions.[32] What is clear is that, whether or not death comes about because it is permitted or because it is actively assisted, it is not uniformly able to be characterized as 'harm'. If this is the case, then unless the distinction between moral responsibility for an act and an omission can be rehabilitated, and in the circumstances of the doctor/patient relationship this seems most unlikely, there is no absolute prohibition in Hippocrates' general statement on assisting in death.

But, of course, Hippocrates then became much more specific, referring directly to the doctor's obligation not to offer active assistance in death. This aversion to active involvement has continued, largely untouched, through the centuries, and although there may be other arguments which could be brought into play to strengthen it, the doctor's first resort is to appeal to the Hippocratic prohibition as the source of his or her antipathy to change in this area. Given what has already been said about the durability of the Oath, this too is worthy of consideration.

The reality of technological advancements means that subtle means have been found to facilitate assistance in ending life, for example switching off life-support machines, withholding or withdrawing treatment and respecting advance directives, all of which are now deemed acceptable practices in certain conditions.

Doctors, therefore, can be seen to be participating in death, albeit passively, where they believe death to be the least bad outcome. This is something that they could not have done in Hippocratic times because the vehicles for doing so were not there. This mirrors to an extent the points made earlier about the performing of surgery or abortions. The Oath addressed a specific culture, a specific time, a specific school of thought and a specific set of capacities. If this is accepted, then the selectivity of adherence to the rules can be challenged on two counts.

First, if the Oath was heavily dependent on practicalities, then its status as a fundamental ethical code can be challenged. Second, if doctors are prepared to dismiss some parts of the code, then a convincing rationale is needed for holding on to other parts of it. In fact, keeping someone alive against his or her wishes, without dignity and often with considerable suffering, may be seen by many as a far greater harm than assisting in death.

Most people desire good health and there is no doubt that its promotion was within the aims of the Hippocratic Oath. The fact that health is such a precious commodity may be one of the reasons why the Hippocratic Oath has survived and allowed doctors' decision-making to go relatively unquestioned. As Daryl Koehn notes: '... the goodness of health explains our willingness to accord doctors authority. If health is something we all desire as a good in itself, and as something of instrumental benefit to all of us as members of the community, then the physician's power to further health is also good.'[33]

The 'good' of health, therefore, stands in direct contrast to the 'bad' of ill-health. As guardians of health, doctors therefore command our respect. Their reliance on the beneficence/non-maleficence constraints derived from the Hippocratic Oath is, therefore, given additional support by the individual's desires and wishes. Arguably, also, the preference for health over ill-health serves to reinforce the status of the doctor, further elevating the power of the code to which he or she proclaims loyalty.

Of course, problems arise when health cannot be achieved. What happens to the professional's role and the Oath then? The Hippocratean writers seemed to be relatively untroubled by this, and the *Prognostic* suggests, 'Now to restore every patient to health is impossible. To do so would have been better even than forecasting the future. But as a matter of fact men do die, some immediately after calling him [the doctor] in ... It is necessary, therefore to learn the natures of such diseases ... and to learn how to forecast them. For in this way you will justly win respect and be an able physician.'[34]

Unfortunately, time and circumstances have reshaped the early and more modest role of the physician into the now familiar, often paternalistic one. No physician can give eternal life to a patient even with modern advances in medicine. But the expectations of the modern patient place a heavy burden upon doctors, and whilst dealing with the pressures of these expectations they must also try to ascertain what can reasonably be accomplished for any particular patient. Whilst realizing that good health is a highly desirable thing, it is equally important to accept that its achievement may not be realizable in all circumstances. Monmeyer addresses this point and suggests that rather than regarding healing as a 'goal' of medical practice, perhaps it would be more appropriate to regard it instead as an 'ideal'. Although he suggests that it should be something 'to be striven for'[35] the ideal should not be an absolute one, for ideals are often impossible to achieve. As he says: 'Ideals are important in medicine, as they are elsewhere in life. Their importance lies in inspiring us to a higher level of commitment to moral practice than we might otherwise be capable of achieving. But there is a down side to ideals as well, and that is if they are too unrealistic, too impossible of attainment, they will distort our perception of what is morally acceptable practice.'[36]

The greatest danger, he feels, is that we will become cynical when medical practice falls short of an ideal. It is time to put away outmoded phrases such as 'doctor knows best' and make decisions that may not be 'just what the doctor ordered'. This conclusion requires, of course, the acceptance of a shift in the balance of power between doctor and patient, and also mandates acceptance that medicine is not a discipline with one goal or outcome. As Koehn notes, 'Some doctors, like members of other professions, are obsessed with controlling and manipulating their environment. It is equally fair to say that some patients share in this obsession. The Hippocratic Oath would not forbid the giving of deadly drugs and abortifacients upon demand if it did not foresee that people would pressure physicians to assist them in committing suicide or aborting a fetus. The Oath prohibits these two activities in particular because these practices have a great potential for luring the doctor away from healing.'[37]

However, the doctor's traditional respect for healing is, as we have shown, intimately linked with the relief of suffering. The fact that doctors are not always able to cure means that they must address the means to achieve this other goal of medicine. When provisions of professional guidelines are inadequate or unclear, the usual practice is to try to interpret what is meant by them. What we have shown, however, is that when difficult and complex decisions have to be made on the borders of medical and professional ethics, they are sometimes made not by a reasoned analysis but rather by a selective interpretation of the Hippocratic Oath's provisions. For example, it may be a relief to deflect decisions concerning assistance with death by stating that the Oath clearly prohibits such practices, but as Monmeyer notes there are other provisions in the Oath which now seem to be conveniently ignored. In addition to those mentioned earlier, these also include the positive requirements of sharing one's wealth with one's teacher, passing on skills to the sons of one's teacher and honouring a variety of Greek gods and goddesses.[38]

Doctors' use of the Hippocratic Oath disguises the fact that, at best, it was a professional agreement designed to lend credibility to the wisdom and teachings of one particular school of medical thought. Admittedly it also contained some 'ethical' prohibitions, but these may have had as much, if not more, to do with the agenda of the time than with any enduring moral commitment. The Oath was not intended to confer any legal obligation, nor perhaps was it foreseen that it would still be referred to in current practice. Rather, it sought to 'stir up the conscience of the individual'.[39] In contemporary medical practice, a wide and complex range of decisions calls for answers unfettered by the provisions of an Oath never intended for such a purpose.

Since the Oath was conceived, increasing medical knowledge and intervention have replaced the elementary practice of medicine which it was designed to control. The simple faith in the healing powers of the doctor has been replaced by the interest of an educated and informed public in the basis of medical decisions, their efficacy and their relevance. The traditional faith invested in doctors has been replaced by a more realistic awareness of their limitations. Yet, despite this, as the controller of health, and given the armoury at the modern doctor's disposal, the pragmatic approach to a doctor's capacities has been superseded by an often unrealistic optimism about what medicine can achieve. This has not only been perpetuated by the medical profession, but patients too are generally happy to endorse such optimism.

In industrialized countries where good diet and hygiene have been secured, more and more emphasis has been placed upon the importance of longevity and, although the restoration, preservation and promotion of health are good and positive things, an absolute commitment to healing may create unrealistic expectations, mandate unwanted technological intervention and impose an onerous burden on the doctor.

Previous experience suggests that doctors appear to adapt to reformations of the Oath and changing legal conditions without losing their professional integrity. The question still to be answered is whether or not there is there any reason to suppose that they cannot continue to do so were they to reassess the Oath's apparent prohibition on actively assisting in death.

There remain many things in the Oath that have contemporary relevance. In its general commitment to doing good the Oath has been echoed in even the most modern statements of medical ethics. But much depends on interpretation. Physicians might, for example, choose to see assisted suicide as a positive act of caring, of relieving suffering. As with the other prohibitions in the Oath which, as we have been seen, have largely been ignored, this final taboo might also come to be viewed as a positive act. Burgess, for example, suggests that 'Caregivers who are frustrated with the failure of medical therapies, palliative efforts and intimate caregiving to yield a life worthy of living can receive some compensation from one final act supporting the suffering person's choice. The memory of their involvement with the person's death might provide some comfort to grieving caregivers.'[40]

Battin echoes these sentiments, noting that what is really important is the reason for the professional's engagement with a patient, noting that 'What is central to the Oath and cannot be deleted without altering its essential character is the requirement that the physician shall come "for the benefit of the sick".'[41] This is a central tenet of modern medicine also, although the notion of 'benefit' has changed.

The modern doctor confronts dilemmas unthought of in the time of Hippocrates. Medicine generates these problems because of its own capacities. Those parts of the Oath which remain relevant might reasonably be said to reflect nothing more than a general commitment to do the best for your patient, an idea which in itself could and should have developed with or without Hippocrates, as it has in other professions. For the rest, the Oath is primarily of historical interest. If calling the Oath into play caused no actual or potential harm, we might be satisfied with its constant reiteration today. However, as in the examples of the prohibition on performing surgery or assisting in death, where adherence to its strictest terms leaves a serious gap between contemporary ethics and historical cant, we would do well to remember that the Oath, as an ethical framework, is fundamentally flawed and provides neither a solid foundation nor convincing argument against assisting patients to end their own lives.

But, it might be said, why **should** doctors be involved in assisted suicide? Once it is conceded that the arguments against assisted death are insufficient to outlaw it, and given that reliance on the Hippocratic Oath as the source of prohibition has been exposed for what it is, this still does not tell us why doctors should be given the authority to act. In what follows, we will show that, since the emphasis has been shifted from doctors' duties to patients' rights, there are indeed good reasons for requiring that only physicians should be empowered to assist in a suicide.

Why Doctors?

A fair death honours the whole life
Outlandish Proverb

When the term assisted suicide or assisted death is used, even
without the prefix 'physician', it is commonly assumed that it will be
a doctor who provides the assistance. As Griffiths notes 'One of the
most striking features of the public euthanasia discussion in the
Netherlands is the generally shared assumption that killing on request
and assistance with suicide must, to be legitimate, be carried out
by a doctor.'[1]

He suggests that one of the main reasons for this assumption is
that many of the necessary reports and examinations in respect of
end-of-life decision-making are carried out by associations and/or
committees within, or related to, the medical profession. It is therefore
taken for granted that, for the process to be appropriate, it has to be
undertaken by the medical profession. His argument continues that

the authoritarian tendencies of the medical profession are reinforced by the law, which also assumes that only the medical profession is competent to deal with the complex decision-making involved and its highly sensitive conclusion.

Although courts have generally treated instances where a spouse or other family member has assisted a person to die with leniency, there is still apparently less discomfort with a death which is assisted by a doctor. Surveys have shown that most people would prefer the doctor to assume ultimate responsibility, although doctors would prefer merely to provide the means for patients to kill themselves (*see Chapter* 5). However, no matter how the final act is done, the doctor is involved one way or the other.

As we have already said, it is, perhaps, scarcely surprising that doctors are more comfortable with assisting death than they are with causing it. However, it is necessary to ask whether or not this is sufficient reason to make a moral or legal distinction between the two, particularly if individuals would prefer the doctor's more active involvement. In any event, it has already been contended that – whether directly or indirectly – doctors **are** involved in the death of their patients. The question posed here is whether or not assistance should be limited to them.

The question is critical for a number of reasons. First, from a positive perspective society has already been critical of the ever-increasing list of what constitutes a 'medical' matter. Would restricting assistance to end life to doctors not merely be adding to the list of human matters which have been medicalized? Secondly, and more negatively, account must be taken of the autonomy of the doctor as well as the autonomy of the patient. We will return to the former question in a moment; first we must look at the autonomy of the doctor in a little more depth.

It is imperative to address the question of the doctor's conscience. It has been argued that the primary value which leads to the conclusion that a change in policy is required is that of autonomy. An interesting feature of our opinion poll and survey was that the public preferred the doctor to carry out the act (euthanasia) by almost the same margins that the doctors preferred the patient to be the final actor (assisted suicide). One interpretation of this finding is that neither group actually wanted to take the final step, and that by a majority they would prefer someone else to do it for them. From the point of view of the public, however, this must not be taken as inferring that the exercise of autonomy is not important. It merely indicates that the autonomy they seek is the autonomy to make the decision and, following on from this, the autonomy to ask for legally available assistance, whatever form that takes.

From the doctor's perspective the autonomy issue may, however, be more complicated. Because of the human feeling that directly killing is worse than not saving life, the doctor's concern will extend beyond the autonomy of the person seeking help and will necessarily impinge on his or her own. The fallacy of the distinction between acts and omissions in philosophical terms has already been exposed, but it none the less understandably remains of concern for those who would be empowered by any change in the law to become involved in the death of another.

It could, of course, be somewhat coldly argued that the emotions of the doctors should be irrelevant. After all, if the rights of the patients are to predominate and if these rights include the right to ask for assistance in dying, then it might be said that the doctor should be obliged to accept this demonstration of autonomy and follow the patient's expressed wishes. It might even be said that doctors are being unnecessarily coy, since they already do participate in the death of their patients. However, neither of these arguments is ultimately convincing.

The right of the patient to seek assistance in death does not necessarily imply a corresponding duty on the doctor to provide it.

WHY DOCTORS?

This is because the right in question is not a 'right to die'. The frequent use of this terminology disguises the real issue. The right of the patient is to ask for help. Even in current law it is clear that the patient cannot demand that doctors provide treatment which is against their conscience or the law or which, in their opinion, is futile or inappropriate. This is a reasonable state of affairs, since doctors are more than mere technicians. They earn the right to call themselves 'professional' because, as with the other professions, they are also expected to exercise discretion, display wisdom and form judgements. Any requirement to act on a patient's request would deny the status of a professional, as well as placing some doctors in a situation where they would have to act directly against their own autonomy rights. For this reason, we do not intend to **require** doctors to assist in a suicide even when it is competently sought. However, we do insist that those who are willing to do so should be enabled to help. This is a reflection of **their** autonomy.

To return to the first question: why should assisted suicide be restricted to doctors? One very obvious answer is that politically and practically it is simpler, and more secure, to draft a law which gives power to the doctor to act on the competent request of a patient. There are a number of reasons for this, perhaps most obviously that the doctor is best qualified, not only in the literal but also in the fullest sense of the word. A choice for death is far from simple. Patients will need to be reassured that they have received all of the relevant information about diagnosis, prognosis, available treatment and other options – for example the availability of palliative care. A 'choice' would not be an autonomous one if, for example, a patient agreed to treatment because relevant information was not provided. Although other considerations will play a part in the patient's choice, clinical expectations are also relevant. Only a doctor can supply this information, and therefore his or her involvement would be a necessary component of any informed decision.

At the level of securing a real choice, therefore, the capacity to exercise personal control in a meaningful sense is predicated on the presence of the doctor as facilitator. To deny the patient access to professional information and advice would be to remove the very rationale for legalization itself, and would render people vulnerable to the uninformed, perhaps biased, views of others.

Ultimately, therefore, if the individual is to act in a self-determining way, he or she needs to have adequate information (even if it is subsequently ignored or only plays a minimal role in his or her final choice). The aim is the attainment of autonomy, which, as Thomasma notes, '... is arguably one of the most cherished values of western civilization, or at least since the Age of reason ... This autonomy has many freedoms, the freedom from obstacles to carry out one's desire; the freedom to know one's options; the freedom to choose goals; the freedom to act; the freedom to commit oneself and the freedom to create.'[2]

Just as it is accepted that a patient who makes a decision **for** treatment without adequate information is not making a true choice, so too, by analogy, the same must hold for decisions which will result in death. The doctor, of course, by virtue of being a professional is not merely the provider of information. The doctor/patient relationship is one which should not simply be based on a consumer model. The information provided will inevitably include evaluation based on professional expertise. In other words, what the doctor can uniquely do is fill in those important parts of the picture which the patient would otherwise lack.

A further argument in favour of law which restricts assistance in dying to doctors is that it would, when coupled with the doctor's professionalism, be less open to abuse than a more widely drafted one. Fear of abuse arguably generates the greatest concern for those who are anxious about changing the law – indeed, even for those who favour change. This fear, which must be treated seriously, generally

WHY DOCTORS?

stems from the concern that an apparent decision for death is not, in fact, a reflection of a real choice. Even where adequate information has been given, there may be still other factors which interfere with the patient's ability truly to make a free choice.

These factors may, for example, include a general concern that the patient who is contemplating such measures is especially vulnerable. Although this has been discussed already (*see Chapter* 1), it is worth repeating briefly here that the elderly or others who are acutely ill may be unusually susceptible to pressures from relatives, even friends, to take the cheaper and 'easier' way out – that is, to 'choose' to die. Quite apart from the doctor's professional commitment to healing where possible, he or she is also relatively speaking disinterested in the decision and therefore considerably less likely to apply any such pressure and more likely to identify it when it has occurred. The doctor's role may also be to act as a gatekeeper in this restricted way to assuage concerns about the too easy ending of a life which was otherwise wanted.

In sum, the very nature of a professional relationship means that the physician's concern can be purely for his or her patient without the burdens, benefits and emotional ties which characterize the relationship between the patient and family or friends. Abuse, in these circumstances, is considerably less likely.

Moreover, the doctor has one further unique qualification – namely, that the practice of medicine is governed by professional and ethical codes. Although it has been pointed out that the doctor's commitment to, for example, the Hippocratic Oath can be described as selective (*see Chapter* 3), there is no doubt that the terms of this and other commitments do have considerable power over doctors. Even taking into account the selective reading of these oaths, as we have already highlighted, there is a core of commonly held values which render the doctor constrained in action. Thus, unlike an individual facing a hard choice for the first, and perhaps only time, the doctor has both a wealth of experience and an ethical position against which to measure his or her behaviour.

Of course, even if respect for patient autonomy is of vital importance to the good practice of medicine, and even if harm need not be interpreted in a simplistic manner, there are some who undoubtedly fear that permitting doctors to act on their patients' request for assisted suicide will so fundamentally change the doctor/patient relationship as to result in a misshapen and foreign practice. Patients will, it is argued, fear doctors as executioners and not healers.[3]

However, this argument, despite its emotional appeal, is intellectually flawed. It has been acknowledged that the doctor's professional ethic is rightly focused on healing and the restoration of health (see Chapter 3), but since this cannot always be achieved we cannot simply say that, at the stage of acknowledging the hopelessness of continued care, the doctor ceases to have a role to play. Indeed, no doctor would accept this as a definition of his or her responsibilities. When cure cannot be effected, and even when pain cannot be alleviated, the doctor still feels him- or herself to have a role to play. What is suggested here is that this role may be more than simply caring in a passive way. Rather, it might be an active and respectful role, taking account of the wishes of the patients themselves and facilitating the death which they want.

In any event, the doctor/patient relationship is not harmed when the doctor acts on the wishes of the patient. Certainly, if the argument were that doctors and not patients should make end-of-life decisions, the relationship **would** be under severe threat, but this is not at the root of arguments for voluntary assisted death. In fact, the doctor/patient relationship may well be enhanced by legal change, since there is clear reason to believe that end-of-life decisions are currently being made, sometimes without the active involvement of the patient (see Chapters 1 and 3). Realistically the patient is much more likely to fear this than to fear the doctor who acts only on request.

WHY DOCTORS?

Increasingly, doctors are showing that they are prepared to respect their patients' views about the kind of healthcare they wish to receive, and are conceding that even a statement which results in a savable life being lost is worthy of some respect. Most notably, this has occurred in those jurisdictions which give legal force to the advance directive or 'living will'. Since these are pre-emptive assertions of patient autonomy, they merit a brief consideration here.

The advance directive is a mechanism whereby people may, in advance of incompetence, direct that certain life-sustaining or life-saving therapy should not be given in certain circumstances. Whether we like it or not, it is clear that some people genuinely fear that they may be unwillingly kept alive as a result of medicine's capacities to prolong existence. For these people, the advance directive provides the opportunity to control, while control is still possible, their future medical care. They have an opportunity for the prospective exercise of autonomy.

The American Euthanasia Society – renamed the Society for the Right to Die – was reactivated in 1974 with the goal of legalizing advance directives through state legislatures. By the end of 1975, bills seeking to give force to such directives had been introduced in 15 states, but passed only in California with the Natural Death Act of 1976. Yet another significant event occurred in the same year, which once again focused the public's mind on end-of-life decisions.[4] Karen Ann Quinlan was a young woman who fell into a coma after ingesting a cocktail of drugs and alcohol. She had stopped breathing and suffered irreparable brain damage, although she was not brain dead and therefore was alive for legal purposes. Three months later her father signed a release to discontinue the use of the respirator which, it was thought, was all that was keeping her alive. Her physicians, however, refused to remove the respirator, saying that to do so would amount to homicide.

The Quinlan family were Catholics and had been advised by priests about the Catholic Church doctrine which distinguishes between acting to take a life and withdrawing treatment which artificially sustains life. Consequently, Joseph Quinlan filed for appointment as Karen's guardian with the express power to authorize discontinuance of all extraordinary means of sustaining vital processes. Noting that Karen was not brain dead, the judge ruled for the hospital. The New Jersey Supreme Court reversed the decision,[5] citing Karen's right to privacy. The respirator was removed, but Karen did not die as expected. She was transferred to a nursing home where she remained in a coma until her death in July 1985. It had taken 10 years for her to die.

This case had a profound effect on both public opinion and legislative activity. As of August 1996, virtually every state in the US now has laws covering advance directives. The widespread legal acceptance that previous choices should be endorsed was recognized throughout the US by the passing of the Patient Self Determination Act 1990, which – broadly speaking – requires all Federal- or Medicaid-funded healthcare facilities to bring to the attention of all patients the state law on advance directives and of their right to make one. Although this statute did not give patients new rights, it vindicated respect for autonomy and may be construed as a facilitation to the making of such directives.

Despite the efforts of numerous pressure groups, and considerable debate, the standing of advance directives in the United Kingdom remains uncertain. Recent cases, however, seem to indicate a clear move towards respecting them. The cases of Re C[6] and Re T[7] suggest that when an informed patient makes a competently executed directive which is both clearly expressed and applies to the circumstances which exist, the doctor would be bound to follow it. Moreover, in the case of Airedale NHS Trust v. Bland,[8] Lord Goff took the opportunity of making the following statement:

It has been held that a patient of sound mind may, if properly informed, require that life support should be discontinued ... the same principle applies where the patient's refusal to give his consent has been expressed at an

earlier date, before he became unconscious or otherwise incapable of
communicating it.[9]

Such cases have gone some way to validating the legal status of
the advance directive. However, despite this, the law has remained
ultimately uncertain, in particular with respect to the extent to which
a doctor is obliged to follow it. The House of Lords Select Committee[10]
also considered this question and recognized that such directives
have **some** legal standing. However, they felt no need to legislate to
clarify the situation, preferring instead that a code was drafted which
would address the directives in all their complexities. The British
Medical Association (BMA) responded and published a Code of
Practice in April 1995.[11]

This Code underlined the importance of such statements in so
far as they encouraged dialogue, allowing patients to express their
wishes concerning future treatment. In the absence of legislative
provision, however, the Code is cautious about the degree to which it
regards these statements as binding. Instead, it goes no further than
to say that a 'requesting statement may reflect an individual's
aspirations and preferences. This can help health professionals
identify how that person would like to be treated *without binding them*
to that course of action, if it conflicts with professional judgement.'[12]

This leaves both patient and doctor confronting ambiguity, but
perhaps the tentative nature of the commitment is explained by what
was clearly a major concern of the BMA. Despite the argument that
the doctor who follows a competent advance directive is – no matter
what sophistry is employed to avoid this conclusion – involved in the
patient's chosen death, the BMA wanted to '... divorce "advance
directives" from practices of euthanasia and assisted suicide and
[place] statements and directives within an accepted framework of
discussion and communication'.[13]

Whatever the remaining reservations about always following the
patient's wishes, the fact that there is a *prima facie* respect given to

advance directives in some countries and an absolute commitment to respecting them in others combines with the points made in earlier chapters to demonstrate that – like it or not – doctors do participate in their patients' deaths. When this is accepted, some of the arguments against medical involvement also disappear.

But it is not necessary to be negative. Doctors are uniquely qualified to give patients the information they need to make an autonomous decision. They are solely responsible for the means which the patient would need to have to hand were an assisted suicide to be undertaken. They are respected professionals whose commitment to saving life will act as a brake on ill-thought-through action and whose commitment to the alleviation of suffering places them centre-stage in vindicating patient choice. Unlike others, who may have personal reasons for acting on a seemingly competent choice for death, doctors are professionally capable of standing back and evaluating the choice with no hope or expectation of personal gain. In other words, the doctor who is willing to help is both best placed to do so and most likely to be trusted to do so. His or her involvement seems likely to ensure that a competent request will be effectuated and to act as a block to the slippery slope which might ensue were other citizens to have the power to act.

Our arguments in favour of restricting assistance in dying to doctors seem also to have been recognized in recent US cases. In the first of these, *Lee* v. *Oregon*,[14] within days of the adoption of the Oregon Death with Dignity Act, opponents of the statute filed injunction proceedings in the United States District Court for Oregon. The Federal courts of the United States have jurisdiction over a state statute which violates the US Constitution. The Federal judge, Judge Hogan, granted the injunction effectively preventing utilization of the law. His judgement rested on his view that the law violated due process of the law because its terms were too vague and placed vulnerable citizens at risk.

WHY DOCTORS?

He also found that the statute denied equal protection under the law, suggesting that certain citizens – for example, those who were terminally ill or depressed – were exposed by it to a risk which was not shared by other citizens, namely the risk of abuse and ultimately an accelerated death sought by third parties hoping to benefit. Furthermore, he found that the requirement in the statute that decisions should be autonomous (competent) – a right protected by the Constitution – was an impermissible burden.

With all respect, this judgement is somewhat strange, and certainly its logic is open to question, particularly since previous court decisions had made it clear that there is a right to refuse medical treatment. Clearly, some of his objections could equally have been applied to this latter situation, as was recognized in the case of *Compassion in Dying* v. *Washington*.[15]

Although dealing with different issues, this case rejected the reasoning and conclusion in *Lee*. The Ninth Circuit Court of Appeals held that the state of Washington could not prohibit physicians from assisting a patient to die. It did not address a specific statutory regime, but found that there was a 'liberty interest' in refusing healthcare and making a choice to die. The court referred extensively to the Supreme Court decisions of *Cruzan*[16] and *Casey*,[17] concluding that if healthcare may be declined with death as the result, positive assistance in bringing about death must also be permissible.

In reaching this conclusion, the court endorsed the argument presented here: that there is no difference between acts and omissions in this situation. Moreover, it translated what for some has been a passive right into an active one. Further, the court declined to conclude that the state had a compelling interest in preserving the lives of those facing terminal illness. Given that there was no state policy preventing suicide, since suicide is not a crime, and that a right exists to refuse life-saving treatment, a total ban on physician assisted suicide could not be upheld.

Finally, the decision in Quill v. Vacco[18] also rejected the reasons offered by the state (in this case, New York) to prevent a physician from assisting a suicide. This judgement adopted a different route from that taken in the Washington case. The court did not use the 'liberty interest' argument – indeed, the court was uncertain about its use in such cases. Rather the court contended that the New York legislation prohibiting assisted suicide denied equal protection under the law.

The court agreed that, although there may be one section of the community facing a terminal illness, in reality this sector is made up of two distinct groups. The first group would be in a hospital, attached to life-support equipment or provided with life-saving therapy. This they could competently refuse to accept, and in this way they would achieve assistance in dying. The second group, however, would not be receiving such treatment and would therefore be unable to attain lawful assistance in their death. In short, one group would be able to die (with assistance, albeit passive) and the other would not. Like Judge Hogan, the Second Circuit found the current law to embrace discrimination, but unlike him, they felt that the discrimination was against those who wished to die.

These cases highlight a number of important points. First, that some courts are disenchanted with the artificiality of the acts/ omissions doctrine. Second, that there is no unanimity concerning what rights people actually have, or at least that there is no agreement about how and when they may be exercised. Third, and most important, they show that in the absence of clear, well-reasoned and unequivocal legislative intervention, there is the potential for abuse on one side of the argument or the other. Moreover, one further step must be noted.

As shown in earlier chapters, attitudes to death and dying do not remain constant. Doctors and patients alike have moved from relatively absolutist opinions to ones which reflect the subtleties and complexities which surround end-of-life decisions. The need for informed debate is clearly shown by these factors, and it is this which we have sought to undertake here. But it must also be borne in mind that in each of the cases highlighted the presumption has been that the person most appropriately authorized to assist in a suicide is the doctor, doubtless for all of the reasons we have identified.

Of course it would be possible to produce a cogent set of arguments which would extend the range of those who could lawfully assist in the death of another. However, for the reasons outlined in this and earlier chapters, it seems unlikely that they would ultimately convince. In the doctor, society has a person skilled, knowledgeable and competent to assist in a genuinely desired death. Moreover, as we have shown, the doctor is already experienced in caring for those who choose death and already acts as proxy. As Palermo says, '... those who better know the value of the total person',[19] including friends, family and so on may be involved, but the ultimate responsibility for acting in what patients believe to be their own best interests is best left to those whose beneficence we do not doubt and whose ability to assist is most clear. With the help of doctors, we may be able to achieve a dignified and 'fair' death.

A Comparative Study

Is it then so terribly wretched a thing to die?
Virgil, *The Aeneid*

The following statements are taken from a 1996 US case, *Quill v. Vacco*[1]

I have a large cancerous tumour which is wrapped around the right carotid artery in my neck and is collapsing my oesophagus and invading my voice box. The tumour has significantly reduced my ability to swallow and prevents me from eating anything but very thin liquids in extremely small amounts. The cancer has metastasized to my plural [sic] cavity and it is painful to yawn or cough ... In early July 1994 I had the [feeding] tube implanted and have suffered serious problems as a result ... I take a variety of medications to manage the pain ... It is not possible for me to reduce my pain to an acceptable level of comfort and to retain an alert state ... At this time, it is clear to me, based on the advice of my doctors, that I am in the terminal phase of this disease ... At the point at which I can no longer endure the pain and suffering associated with my cancer, I want to have drugs available for the purpose of hastening my death in a humane and certain manner. I want to be able to discuss freely with my treating physician my intention of hastening my death through the consumption of drugs prescribed for that purpose.

Jane Doe, a 76-year-old retired physical education instructor

In May 1992, I developed a Kaposi's sarcoma skin lesion. This was my first major illness associated with AIDS. I underwent radiation and chemotherapy to treat this cancer ... In September 1993, I was diagnosed with cytomegalovirus (CMV) in my stomach and colon which caused severe diarrhoea, fevers and wasting ... In February 1994, I was diagnosed with microsporidiosis, a parasitic infection for which there is effectively no treatment ... At approximately the same time, I contracted AIDS-related pneumonia. The pneumonia's infusion therapy was so extremely toxic that I vomited with each infusion ... I have begun to lose bowel control ... For each of these conditions I have undergone a variety of medical treatments, each of which has had significant adverse side-effects ... While I have tolerated some [nightly intravenous] feedings, I am unwilling to accept this for an extended period of time ... I understand that there are no cures ... I can no longer endure the pain and suffering and I want to have drugs available for the purpose of hastening my death.

William A Barth, a 28-year-old former fashion editor

The ultimate success of this case shows that even the law is increasingly uneasy with prohibiting assistance in dying. Yet resistance remains to grasping the nettle. In this chapter we will show, however, that civilized countries can and have faced up squarely to the paucity of arguments against physician assistance in death without bringing their communities to a standstill, and without being banished from the community of civilization.

In the US, the development of legislation and societal attitudes towards suicide has generally tended to parallel that of Britain. This is further reflected in respect of assisted suicide, as American ethical literature, professional bodies and the law have traditionally condemned physician assisted suicide. For example, in 1973, the American Medical Association (AMA) concluded that the intentional termination of life is contrary to medical professional standards and the policy of the AMA.[2] Nearly 20 years later, the AMA reiterated their position when their council on Ethical and Judicial Affairs stated that 'the physician should not intentionally cause death.'[3]

However, studies show that this may no longer be in line with public opinion. A large majority of Americans fully endorse recent legal changes granting terminally ill patients, and sometimes their families, the option of accelerating their death by refusing or terminating treatment.[4] Other evidence shows that the majority of Americans favour physician assisted suicide for the terminally ill. For example, in April 1990 the Roper Report found that 64 per cent of Americans believe that the terminally ill should have the right to request and receive physician assistance in dying.[5]

Washington, California and Oregon have all held referenda on proposals to allow physicians to help terminally ill, competent adults commit suicide. They narrowly failed in Washington and California, gaining 46 per cent of the vote. Only in Oregon did voters approve the proposal – by a vote of 51 per cent to 49 per cent in November 1994. This will be discussed in more depth later.

Meantime it is striking that we could find no reported American case of a doctor being criminally sanctioned for helping a patient hasten his or her own death. In the case of Dr Timothy Quill,[6] he prescribed barbiturates to a 45-year-old patient suffering from acute myelomonocytic leukaemia, which allowed her to end her life. Dr Quill was not successfully prosecuted. Even in the notorious case of Dr Jack Kevorkian, prosecution has been unsuccessful.

As with many other countries, underneath the official legal condemnation of physician assisted suicide is a strong undercurrent of the time-honoured but hidden practice of doctors helping terminally ill patients to hasten their deaths.[7] Increasingly, doctors are now admitting this practice.[8] It therefore appears that not only is public opinion changing but, perhaps because of the evident leniency with which the law treats such cases, the opinions of medical professionals are also changing towards a more open attitude to discussing the practice of assisting a patient to die.

After Dr Quill's case was heard, he and his colleagues proposed clinical criteria for physician assisted suicide.[9] The main provisions are as follows:[10]

1   *The patient must have a condition that is incurable and associated with severe, unrelenting suffering.*
2   *The physician must ensure that the patient's suffering and the request are not the result of inadequate comfort care.*
3   *The patient must clearly, repeatedly, and of his or her own free will and volition request to die.*
4   *The physician must be sure that the patient's judgement is not distorted.*
5   *Physician assisted suicide must be carried out only in the context of a meaningful doctor/patient relationship.*
6   *The physician must consult with another experienced physician.*
7   *The physician must document the case.*

This represents but one set of criteria which might act to circumscribe the behaviour of the maverick, and admittedly it is not without its problems. However, it has the merit of addressing four square some of the concerns which are traditionally expressed by those opposing assisted suicide. But, of course, in the US the difficulty of translating any set of principles into practice may be compounded by factors which are peculiar to the state concerned. The first country in the world to tolerate assisted suicide and euthanasia was the Netherlands, where debate began some time ago.

Since 1886, euthanasia has been defined in the Penal Code of the Netherlands as an intentional act to terminate life by a doctor on the urgent request of the patient. Assisted suicide is also defined in the Penal Code as the intentional assistance given to a person to terminate his or her life upon that person's request. Article 294 of the Penal Code makes it an offence to assist another to commit suicide. The Code contains in article 293 a specific prohibition on killing another even 'at that person's express and serious request' which 'will be punished by imprisonment of at the most 12 years or a fine of the fifth category'. Article 40 of the Penal Code allows the courts the possibility of adopting the exception created in the legislation in cases of *force majeure,* or necessity.

In a series of cases dating from the case of 'Leeuwarden' in 1973 and culminating in a decision of the Supreme Court (Hoge Raad) in the 'Alkmaar'[11] case of 1984, the Dutch courts have held that the defence of necessity takes two forms: first 'psychological compulsion' and secondly 'emergency' (*noodtoestand*) – the distinction between being psychologically overborne on the one hand and, on the other, choosing to break the law in order to promote a higher good.

A legal consensus has emerged from these decisions that a physician can invoke a defence of necessity if he or she acts at the explicit request of the patient who, until recently, was usually incurably and terminally ill and experiencing prolonged and unacceptable suffering. This means that, in practice, physicians will not be prosecuted provided they can prove that they have followed certain guidelines. Such immunity from prosecution applies only to doctors and to no one else (*see Chapter 4*).

The circumstances in which a person who performs euthanasia or assisted suicide can rely on this defence have been summarized as follows:

1 *The request for euthanasia must come only from the patient and must be entirely free and voluntary.*
2 *The patient's request must be well considered, durable and persistent.*
3 *The patient must be experiencing intolerable (but not necessarily*

physical) *suffering, with no prospect of improvement. The 'not
necessarily physical' condition was endorsed by the most recent ruling of
the Dutch supreme court in June 1994.*[12]

4   *Euthanasia must be a last resort. Other alternatives to alleviate the
    patient's situation must have been considered and found wanting.*

5   *Euthanasia must be performed by a physician.*

6   *The physician must consult with an independent physician colleague
    who has experience in this field.*

But before the Dutch reached this conclusion, the debate had
been intense. In 1959, the Royal Dutch Medical Association stated in
its Guidelines of Medical Ethics that doctors were never allowed to act
with the purpose of shortening life. They were also not allowed to
withhold the care needed to preserve life. The rationale was simply
that it was not the doctor's task to judge the meaning of life itself. But
in 1968, discussion about euthanasia was brought into the spotlight
by a book entitled *Recent Medical Ethical Thinking*.[13]

The Dutch Parliament first became involved in the discussion of
euthanasia in 1970. They set up a Commission of the Health Council
with the remit of ascertaining whether it was ever acceptable to
intervene in the ending of life. In 1971 the first euthanasia case was
brought before the court. A doctor helped her mother die by
administering a lethal dose of morphine. The legal outcome, which
was a one-year suspended sentence with one year probation, turned
the discussion into a public debate. Immediately after this case, the
Dutch Society for Voluntary Euthanasia was founded. The main
purpose of this Society was to encourage a social acceptance of
voluntary euthanasia and to promote its legalization.

In 1982 the Dutch Health Council reported their conclusions on
the issue of euthanasia and, on the basis of their findings, two years
later in 1984 the Royal Dutch Medical Association published their
opinion. They concluded that if assistance was to be provided to end
a person's life, then such assistance was to be carried out only by a

qualified physician. The Dutch Medical Association then set out criteria for physicians to follow, which were similar to those already laid down by the courts.

The Report lists five conditions

1   *The patient must make a voluntary request.*
2   *The request must be well considered.*
3   *The wish for death must be durable.*
4   *The patient must be in unacceptable suffering.*
5   *The physician must consult with a colleague who must agree with the proposed course of action.*

In the meantime, several proposals were made to reform the law prohibiting euthanasia and assisted suicide. From the mid-1980s onwards, one of the central questions in Dutch political debate was whether euthanasia should be legalized altogether, as proposed by some members of the Dutch Parliament, or should remain a criminal act in principle, but with clear rules about when prosecution should not take place.

The official definition of euthanasia appears in the Report of the Dutch Government Commission on Euthanasia. This was published in 1985 and defined euthanasia as 'A deliberate termination of an individual's life at that individual's request, by another. Or, in medical practice, the active and deliberate termination of a patient's life, on that patient's request, by a doctor.'[14] This makes it clear that in the Netherlands the word 'euthanasia' is synonymous with **voluntary euthanasia**, because it has to be requested by the person wishing it.

Once the basic criteria had been established, there were still many outstanding issues to be addressed. For example, under what conditions could a request for euthanasia be validly made? When the criteria were first being applied, a patient usually had to be terminally ill before his or her case would be considered. Current discussion in the Netherlands is centred on whether this is still the case, or whether a request for euthanasia may be validly considered if the patient's suffering results from something other than a terminal illness. A recent court decision (the *Chabot* case[15]) has given an indication that the latter may have also become accepted.

This case is of particular interest for several reasons. First because it is a recent judgement (1994) which went to the Dutch Supreme Court, secondly because it concerns physician assisted suicide rather than euthanasia, and thirdly because it broadens the circumstances under which euthanasia and assistance with death can be given. Furthermore, it provides a recent example of how the procedures, safeguards and rules are applied in practice in the Netherlands.

The case centred around a woman who was not physically ill nor, arguably, incurably ill; but she had an intense wish to end her life. She had already saved up anti-depressant drugs in an unsuccessful attempt to commit suicide, and was afraid to try again in case a second failure would result in either her committal or her survival in a debilitated state.

The defendant, Dr Chabot, supplied a lethal dose of drugs which the woman consumed in the presence of the defendant, a family doctor (note, not the woman's family doctor), and a friend. Dr Chabot was subsequently accused of the offence of assisting her suicide.

The woman had had a tragic life. She had an unhappy and violent marriage but doted on her two sons. She was devastated when her eldest son committed suicide, and wanted to die herself. Only caring for her younger son prevented her from doing so. She was hospitalized for a brief period for psychiatric treatment. The treatment appeared to be unsuccessful. Her father died, and she divorced her husband shortly afterwards. Her youngest son was then involved in a car accident; during his treatment in hospital doctors discovered a malignant tumour in his lung. He died six months later, and it was on the evening of this death that the woman made her attempt to kill herself.

During this period she had written several letters in an effort to obtain the appropriate drugs to kill herself. The Dutch Society for Voluntary Euthanasia gave her Dr Chabot's address. She persisted in refusing any therapy and Dr Chabot consulted seven of his colleagues. According to six out of the seven consulted, this woman's suffering was without any prospect of improvement.

The court concluded that the suffering was durable, without any prospect of recovery and that the woman's request to die was well founded and freely made with a good insight into the consequences and her situation.

As Griffiths noted in his translation of the facts of the case heard in the Court of Appeals, 'Although her condition was in principle treatable, treatment would probably have been long and the chance of success was small. None of the experts consulted considered that there was in fact any realistic treatment perspective in light of her well established refusal of treatment.'[16]

On appeal, however, the Dutch Supreme Court found the defendant guilty. However, they did uphold the important point that the very nature of the defence of 'necessity' does not limit suffering to merely that which is somatic or terminal. The problem in this case appeared to be the sufficiency of evidence, for the deceased was not actually examined by a second psychiatrist. Thus the defence of necessity was rejected and the defendant found guilty. Implicitly, all the other arguments in favour of acceptance of *force majeure*, or necessity, were accepted. Interestingly, although a conviction was secured, 'the person of the defendant and the circumstances in which the offence was committed ... have led the Supreme Court to apply Article 9a of the Criminal Code and not to impose any punishment or other measure.'[17]

In summary, then, the Supreme Court held that:

1 *Assisted suicide is legally justifiable for a patient whose suffering is not somatic or terminal.*

2   A person who is suffering from a psychiatric disorder can make an
     autonomous, voluntary and competent request to die.

Whether or not this judgement may steepen any perceived
'slippery slope' is beyond conjecture here. What the judgement does
do is broaden the circumstances under which assistance with death
is permissible in the Netherlands. Related to this is a move away from
a rigid and preconceived idea of what amounts to suffering, to a more
flexible and patient-centred determination. Whatever the
interpretation, the case will certainly add to the debate which has
been going on openly in the Netherlands for about 30 years. There is
still a long way to go before consensus is reached.

Over the years, Dutch legislative developments were piecemeal,
the result of a wide variety of research and expertise. The true
number of deaths due to euthanasia in the Netherlands was, until a
few years ago, not known. Estimates differed and were often based
upon questionable factual material or on small numbers of
observations. The need for information about the actual occurrence
of euthanasia prompted an investigation by the Commission of
Inquiry into the Medical Practice concerning Euthanasia. During 1990
and 1991 an investigation into medical decisions concerning the end
of life was undertaken in the Netherlands upon request of the
Commission of Inquiry.[18] A study of this size had never been
previously attempted, and physicians' apparent willingness to
respond gave a valuable insight into one of the most sensitive aspects
of their medical practice.

The results of the study were not only to be a contribution to
legislative developments on euthanasia and assisted suicide, but also
provided information and contributed to the much broader public
discussion surrounding general medical decision-making at the end
of life.

The study shows[19] that euthanasia was performed in 1.8 per cent
of all deaths. Euthanasia was performed by general practitioners in

two thirds of these cases. In terms of absolute numbers, this means that in the year 1990 about 2,300 cases of euthanasia occurred, and that euthanasia was carried out by general practitioners in 1,550 of these cases (2.9 per cent of all deaths in general practice). Specialists performed euthanasia in the remaining cases (1.4 per cent), with the exception of some 20 cases where it was performed by nursing home physicians.

Although euthanasia is a criminal act according to Dutch law, prosecutions have tended to be rare provided physicians abide by strict rules. However, because of the sensitivity of the issues involved, some physicians have been reluctant accurately to attribute a cause of death to euthanasia on the death certificate. In 1990 the Royal Dutch Medical Association and the Ministry of Justice agreed upon a notification procedure which contains the following criteria:

1. *The physician performing euthanasia or assisted suicide does not issue a declaration of a natural death but informs the local medical examiner of the circumstances by filling out an extensive questionnaire.*
2. *The medical examiner reports to the district attorney.*
3. *The district attorney then decides whether or not a prosecution should be instituted.*

This notification procedure was laid down in regulations under the Burial Act and acquired legal status in 1994.

Although doctors performing euthanasia or assisted suicide will probably not be prosecuted if it is performed according to these guidelines, the doctor who terminates the life of a patient following his or her explicit and repeated request does so within very strict parameters, which also encompass a respect for the patient's self-determination. For example, the patient must be made aware of the diagnosis and prognosis of his or her condition, therapeutic possibilities and all other relevant information.

However satisfactory the Dutch position, and although economic and cultural similarities can be found in many Western countries, there are factors which make its direct translation into other countries problematic. One very important consideration is the way in which healthcare is delivered. Healthcare systems differ widely, especially in the financing of patient care. An effective healthcare insurance system in the Netherlands and the National Health Service in Britain ensure that the majority of people who go into hospital do not need to worry about who is going to foot the bill. This is not the case in the US, where there is no universal access to healthcare. A long-term illness usually involves extensive medical treatment and, at the end of life, a month in an American hospital may cost $60,000 or more, consuming a modest lifetime estate in 30 days.[20] Although this is enough to give the patient concern, of greater concern is often the financial burden that may be placed on the patient's family.

Therefore, there is a recurring fear in the US that economic considerations may play an influential role in turning a 'right' to die into an obligation to do so. This fear is not without grounds. Studies have shown that 60 per cent of those interviewed said they would consider assisted death rather than being a financial burden on their children or other people as they grow older.[21]

There are also other factors which militate against a direct translation of one particular system to another country. Again, to compare the Netherlands with the US, one hurdle is the nature of the doctor/patient relationship, which overall is quite different. Doctors in the US have unique and complex professional and ethical dilemmas. For example, a doctor knowing of his patient's lack of funds may suggest assistance to end the patient's life as opposed to expensive and possibly futile treatment. The doctor may also be subjected to external pressures, for example from insurance companies or hospital boards trying to keep medical costs down. In addition to this, professional practice is changing and American doctors seem less inclined to treat people because of potential litigation, irrespective of whether they could pay for treatment or not.[22]

Secondly, although America may be regarded as a 'melting pot' of different cultures and races, the Dutch claim that it is the egalitarian nature of their own society which is the cornerstone of their policies on end-of-life assistance; a patient's self-determination is always respected. As Admiraal suggests:

Social development in the Netherlands over the last decades has led to an increase in the value placed on shared decision making and openness, leading to a situation where patients now have a legal right of access to their health records ... In other words, in the Netherlands every patient has the right to the most advanced treatment, the right to refuse even that treatment and the indisputable right to judge his or her own suffering and to request euthanasia. In these ways, it may be thought that the Netherlands is considerably ahead of other countries where the medical profession remains paternalistic in respect of its patients.[23]

Thirdly, the fact that the US is one of the most aggressively litigious countries in the world is not conducive to sensitive discussion between patient and doctor, particularly where doubt about the legality of assisted death remains.

It seems to be the case that the doctor/patient relationship in the Netherlands is a more open one. There is easier, and therefore more frequent access to individual practitioners, which leads to better communication than is the case in multi-practice or hospital outpatient facilities in the US, where building a doctor/patient relationship is more difficult and such relationships tend to be more unequal.

Lastly, the type of doctor/patient relationship may influence where a person may die and ultimately how much control a person has over the time and circumstances of the death. For example, hospitalization may make people more vulnerable to control. Unknown surroundings and interventions and unfamiliar doctors may make discussions about end-of-life assistance intolerably difficult. A recent study by Miles and Gomez suggests that around 85 per cent of deaths in the US take place in healthcare institutions,[24] whereas in the

Netherlands, if aggressive treatment has failed, many people go home to be with their families to die, and assistance to die is provided by the family physician.[25]

Despite these differences, Battin[26] suggests that America's culture supports and promotes self-analysis, allowing inward scrutiny of one's own motives as well as those of others. Such analysis, she feels, would best facilitate the practice of physician assisted suicide in preference to all other methods which end life. Thus, the practical adoption of the Dutch model may be unlikely, but the tenets which underpin it are as much part of the culture of the US as they are of the Netherlands.

That the US **is** able to adopt radical views on assisted death is clear from the recent legislation in the state of Oregon. The bill which resulted in this law was introduced by the citizens' initiative process. This was the same process that was used unsuccessfully in both Washington in 1990[27] and California in 1992.[28] When the Washington initiative was defeated, apparently many people predicted that the issue would resurface, probably in Washington or Oregon, because initiative petitions appear on the ballots regularly in these states. By securing the signatures of 6 per cent of registered voters who have voted in previous elections, Oregon citizens can have an initiative placed on a state-wide ballot.

So why was the initiative successful in Oregon? The initial polls showed that the Washington and California initiatives were very well supported. Washington was ahead 62 per cent to 28 per cent in the early polls; California 71 per cent to 21 per cent.[29] However, these leads disappeared very quickly. Both measures were portrayed as flawed, and as going too far, since they would have legalized not only physician assisted suicide but voluntary active euthanasia as well. It was felt that the chances of abuse were too great. The differences do not, however, appear to comprise purely technical drafting problems but may also reflect a more fundamental difference in culture.

The Catholic Church in Washington and California embarked on
a massive and expensive negative advertising campaign, and the
doctors within the California and Washington State Medical
Associations actively opposed the measures.

By comparison, Oregonians seemed to adopt a more 'free spirit'
culture coupled with a strong libertarian streak. For example, the
Oregon Medical Association voted to remain officially neutral
regarding the initiative; this seems to have been critical to its success.
In addition, the Oregon Hospice Association 'missed an opportunity
to get their message out',[30] being unable to reach agreement
concerning policies on palliative care. This seems also to have been
the case with the churches, who failed to take a united front. This in a
state where 10 per cent of the community are members of the
Catholic Church, the largest denomination in Oregon. Cheryl Smith,
Legal Services Director at the Oregon Rehabilitation Association and
primary drafter of the Oregon Death With Dignity Act, agrees that,
overall, the main opponents' neutrality and divisiveness were pivotal
to the initiative's success, and that they may even have been viewed
as tacitly supporting the measure.

One positive thing that does appear to have been a byproduct of
this legislation, regardless of the result of the current appeals against
it, is that terminally ill patients seem to have begun to benefit from
the Oregon medical community's attempts to improve compassionate
and effective care at the end of life.[31] Further evidence of this is that
the medical school at the University of Oregon is creating a new
multi-disciplinary Comfort Care Team and now offers courses on
comfort care for the dying, making comfort care an academic
speciality.

The main features and safeguards of measure 16, as adopted by
the Oregon legislature, are as follows:

1 *The doctor must determine that the person is terminally ill, competent
   and making a decision that is both voluntary and informed.*

2   The doctor must obtain a second opinion on the patient's diagnosis, voluntariness, capability and informed decision-making.

3   If either of the physicians believes that the patient is suffering from some sort of mental illness which could affect his or her judgement, the patient must be referred for counselling.

4   The patient must be advised of the diagnosis, prognosis and other alternatives, including comfort care.

5   The physician must specifically ask the patient to notify his or her next of kin.

6   The patient must make one written and two oral requests.

7   The patient is free to change his or her mind at any time, and the physician must give the patient a final opportunity to withdraw the request.

8   Waiting periods of 15 days between the initial oral request and the writing of the prescription, and 48 hours between the written request and the writing of the prescription, must elapse.

9   All information must be documented in the medical records.

10   The Act is only applicable to Oregon residents.

11   The Health Division is required to review its records annually.

12   Wills and contracts may not be conditioned on requests under the Act.

13   Insurance or annuity policies may not be conditioned.

14   Mercy killing, lethal injection and active euthanasia are not authorized.

Cheryl Smith[32] says that the principal difference between measure 16 and previous proposals is that it is purely a prescribing bill. The law does not expressly allow a physician to administer a lethal injection. Therefore it is the patient who is required to perform the final action that brings about death.

This is one of the major differences between Oregon's law and the first piece of legislation in the world to authorize active voluntary euthanasia.

On 22nd February 1995, a Private Member's bill was introduced to the Northern Territory of Australia's Parliament. After 16 hours of debate, the Rights of the Terminally Ill Act was passed in Australia's Northern Territory by 15 votes to 10, on 25th May 1995. It came into force on 1st July 1996.

Again, it is interesting to ask why the act was successfully passed in the Northern Territory. Before considering the reasons, there are some general points which can be made about Australia.

Unlike the US, Australia has free universal access to healthcare. Australians may also be said to have a similar 'free spirit' to that which, it has been suggested, applies in the state of Oregon. Public opinion also seems to be in favour of voluntary euthanasia. The Roy Morgan Research Centre conducted a poll in July 1995 which showed that 78 per cent of the Australian public were in favour of allowing doctors to perform euthanasia if requested by a hopelessly ill patient in great pain.[33]

More specific to the Northern Territory, however, was the fact that its Chief Minister, Marshall Perron, himself tabled the bill and his high profile and personal credibility did much to promote the bill.

Related to this, like Oregon, the Northern Territory may be regarded as having a conducive legislative procedure. They do not use the citizen's initiative but they have only 25 people in their legislative assembly, and no further institutions to check legislative processes.[34]

This is not to say there was no opposition. Unlike the situation in Oregon, religious lobbying groups were organized and exerted intense pressure against the Northern Territory's bill. A similar pattern can be seen with regard to the Northern Territory's branch of the Australian Medical Association, who formed a main opposing lobby group.

The main features and safeguards of the bill are as follows:

1   *The person has to be terminally ill.*[35]
2   *The person has to be a mentally competent adult, aged 18 or over.*
3   *The person must be 'experiencing pain, suffering and/or distress to an extent unacceptable to the patient'.*
4   *The patient must make a written request to a medical practitioner for assistance in terminating his or her life.*

A COMPARATIVE STUDY

5   The patient must have received counselling on the nature of the illness, its prognosis and medical treatment, including palliative care, that is available.

6   The doctor must be satisfied that the patient not only has a 'terminal illness' but is experiencing 'severe pain and suffering' which no available medical treatment could cure.

7   A second medical opinion must be obtained from a practitioner with qualifications in dealing with the mentally ill. He or she must examine the patient and certify that the patient is not suffering from 'a treatable clinical depression in respect of the illness'.

8   Palliative care must not be reasonably available. If it is available it must alleviate the patient's pain and suffering to levels acceptable to him or her.

9   There must be a seven-day 'cooling off' period before the authorization is signed, plus a 48-hour period before the lethal injection or other measure is administered.

It is interesting to note that, unlike Oregon, it is not necessary to be resident in the Northern Territory for the act to apply.

In an attempt to pacify the bill's critics, a number of additional safeguards were introduced. These include:

1   a definition of terminal illness, to include injury or derangement of mental or physical faculties

2   the addition of the requirement that there must be no treatment available to effect a cure

3   the need for a second doctor who is not a relative, and holds diplomas in psychological medicine or its equivalent, to certify the illness and that the patient is not suffering from a treatable clinical depression in respect of the illness, plus a third doctor if neither of the other two is an expert in palliative care.

It has been suggested that these additional safeguards render the law effectively unworkable and make it even harder for patients to receive assistance with death than before the legislation was introduced. In particular, the new safeguards seem to include the need for a plethora of medical specialists, and these specialists have to be residents of the Northern Territory. Given that the population of the Northern Territory is less than 200,000, and that the Territory has only five psychiatrists and no cancer specialist,[36] it is not going to be easy to meet the terms of the legislation. However, despite such difficulties, in September 1996 the first assisted death did take place in the Northern Territory.

The international picture, then, represents a variety of styles and cultural influences. However, those countries which have acted to permit (in one form or another) assistance in dying have addressed and reconciled themselves with the arguments for and against choice at the end of life. No matter the healthcare system, no matter the jurisprudence, ultimately steps have been taken to respect autonomy in death as in life.

However, obstacles still remain in other countries. Despite the fact that some countries have already accepted that there are convincing arguments in favour of legalizing assisted suicide, others, like the UK, remain reluctant to concede this. Although UK law is equally subject to the charge that failure to move for legalization is inconsistent in the light of what is already permitted, the attitude of legislators and others has yet to reflect the consistency which can be expected of a legal system.

It may be intelligible that politicians are reluctant to take a firm stand in this highly sensitive area, but their fears about electoral consequences, which may play a part in this reluctance, are not necessarily borne out by research. Recently, the British Medical Association asked 750 doctors the following question: 'Do you believe doctors should be legally permitted to actively intervene to end the life of a terminally ill patient, where the patient, when competent, has made a witnessed request for euthanasia?' The results were that 46 per cent said yes, 44 per cent no.[17] Our own

A COMPARATIVE STUDY

surveys of the public and doctors/pharmacists add weight to the
contention that the law is now out of step with contemporary
morality.

In a survey of 986 adult members of the Scottish general public
who were questioned in January 1996, 67 per cent agreed that the law
should be changed to allow assisted death. Of that number, 42 per
cent said they would prefer voluntary euthanasia, while 28 per cent
preferred physician assisted suicide and 22 per cent showed no
preference for either option. Just over half the sample agreed that
physician assisted suicide should be made legal in Scotland, and
when asked if 'Human beings should have the right to choose when to
die', 67 per cent overall agreed that this should be the case.

The second survey was a postal survey of healthcare
professionals including hospital physicians, general practitioners,
surgeons, psychiatrists, pharmacists and anaesthetists. The results
were calculated on the basis of 1,000 responses (which, interestingly,
represented 50 per cent of the questionnaires sent out). Sixty per cent
had treated a patient who was considering suicide, and 28 per cent
had been asked to provide the means for a patient to kill him- or
herself. Four per cent said that they had provided the means (such as
drugs or information about lethal acts) to assist a patient to kill him-
or herself. Fifty-four per cent said they were in favour of a change in
the law to allow physician assisted suicide in specific circumstances.
Forty-three per cent said that they found physician assisted suicide
preferable to euthanasia (more or less the opposite to the preferences
of the public), although a high proportion of the sample were in the
'don't know/not stated' category (38 per cent).

There was little by way of difference in the percentages of hospital
physicians, medical GPs, surgeons or psychiatrists favouring a change
in the law, with approximately 48 per cent in favour (this was still a
higher percentage than those who were actively opposed to legalization).
This was in sharp contrast to the percentage of pharmacists, 72 per

cent of whom were in favour, and the anaesthetists, of whom 56 per cent were in favour.

For those who, even in the face of legislative change in some countries, remain concerned that legalizing assisted suicide is of dubious morality, let us return to the case with which we started this chapter. Despite their appalling suffering and despite the great courage shown by those who challenged the current law, those involved were denied the right to act on their convictions. Although the US Supreme Court found in favour of the three plaintiffs on 2nd April 1996, none of them lived to see their struggle vindicated. As with many others, they were denied this final chance to assert their dignity. It can only be hoped that their courage will inspire their loved ones and that in some way their unfinished battle will be of benefit to others.

A Good Death

If I must die,
I will encounter darkness as a bride
And hug it in mine arms
Shakespeare, *Measure for Measure*

The desire for a good death is both common and rational. As the taboos about discussing death break down, as people live longer and have time to contemplate the end of their lives, and as medicine holds out more and more possibilities, the desire to take control becomes greater. No longer satisfied with the lottery of life, no longer obsessed with quantity rather than quality, we are liberated to encapsulate our death as a part of who we are as human beings. A culture which values freedom and autonomy is a culture which encourages personal development and personal choice.

Stripped of its fear, death becomes yet one more reflection of our lives, and the manner of our death a statement about the values with which we have lived. Consciously or otherwise, the knowledge that life must end helps to shape our moral and social adaptation. Whether or not we believe in an afterlife, the parameters of inevitability give meaning and content to what we do and who we are. As Dougherty says: 'In one sense, dying is the most personal and private of all events. Each of us comes to the end of a unique life and dies his or her own death. Along with birth, death sets the natural boundaries of a particular life's trajectory. But unlike birth, the consciousness of death can define a person's plan of life. In existential terms, the consciousness of an inevitable personal death provokes an anxiety which is radically individualizing. The fact of my death makes this my life.'[1]

The desire to claim one's death as part of one's life choices is rapidly becoming one of the most compelling and frequently used arguments in favour of permitting choice at the end of life. As we have shown, this is a clear reflection of the contemporary emphasis (at least in Western culture) on concepts such as autonomy, respect for persons, and dignity. As Gunderson and Mayo say: 'The richest sense of dignity is the notion of being worthy of respect by virtue of being able to conduct one's life autonomously, that is, according to principles freely chosen or in accord with one's own authentic values.'[2]

The question we have posed is essentially why, if we are entitled to respect in life, we should not be entitled to that same respect when life approaches its end. If a dignified life is a good life, why is a good death not a dignified one also? Our answer is clear: There are clearly entrenched, and often flawed, arguments used to steal away from those who want or need it the right to vindicate their own values at this most private time. Once exposed, these arguments carry little weight, and certainly they do not defeat the arguments in favour of permitting choice. The fact that I might fear my own death is insufficient for me to insist that others do too, that there is not for them a time when death is preferred.

In fact, of course, as we have also shown, this is already conceded by societies and by laws. But the final step – the one which would truly liberate the individual – sticks in the throat of those who control our lives. Is this based on paternalism? Possibly. Is it rooted in our own fears of death? Probably. Is it derived from some imagined fear about the breakdown of society? More than likely. What it is *not* grounded in is respect. Saints and philosophers from Thomas More to Francis Bacon, David Hume and Jeremy Bentham have endorsed the right to choose death and to do so with assistance if necessary. It seems implausible to suggest that their views represent or would lead to the end of civilization as we know it. What history shows is that communities are capable of accommodating general prohibitions on killing, whilst at the same time admitting of exceptions to the general rule. And some modern societies have been courageous enough to translate this into reality. That is all that we seek here.

The first taboo to go, of course, fell with the decriminalization of suicide. Of course, it might be said that there is a clear difference between this and decriminalizing assisted suicide. The difference could be said to be twofold. First, that a third party is involved in the latter and, second, that allowing that third party to help another to die would weaken society to such an extent that it would become callous, uncaring and disrespectful of life. These arguments need to be addressed, but, we would suggest, they are as defeasible as the ones discussed earlier.

Third-party involvement is a legitimate concern for the third parties. We have already explored why we believe that assistance in dying is best left to doctors; the arguments need not be restated. But, of course, it is equally not our intention to impose involvement. Although doctors already are involved in the death of some patients, the fact that they see a difference between 'letting die' and providing the means for a patient's suicide, even if ethically dubious, is worthy of attention. For that reason, just as in other highly contentious matters which bear on personal morality, it is likely that any legislation designed to permit physician assisted suicide would incorporate a 'conscience clause', allowing those with moral objections to refuse to participate. That doctors may feel more guilt about doing something active is understood, but it in no way affects the morality of the act itself. As Rachels says, '... we cannot validly argue that a form of conduct is wrong, or that one type of behaviour is worse than another, because of feelings of guilt or innocence.'[3]

In any event, we have already shown that if we are not to discriminate against people on the grounds of their clinical condition, then we must honestly concede that the distinction between killing and letting die is an intellectual and moral nonsense, not least because even in the latter case there already **is** third-party involvement. The patient who refuses life-sustaining treatment renders his or her carers, when this refusal is accepted, complicit in his or her death. Care continues, even if it is directed at alleviating the process of dying rather than at cure. No doctor or nurse may insist upon treating those who have competently rejected therapy, no matter what his or her views are as to the rationality or the morality of the choice.

But where the person either cannot commit suicide or has no life-saving treatment which can be refused, he or she is no less entitled to the 'good' death which is sought, and can be achieved, by others. The doctor or nurse who assists in this case is no more complicit in death than his or her colleagues in the first situation. Clearly, if the statistical evidence is to be believed, some healthcare professionals have already reached this conclusion by themselves and, in defiance of the law but in line with their assessment of morality, have bravely and compassionately acted to remove this false differentiation (*see Chapter 5*).

Of course, it is tempting to stay firmly rooted in the past, to fail to take account of morality as a shifting phenomenon. To be sure, the central tenets of ethics may remain substantially the same over time, but their content can and does change. For many at the time, for example, morality was able easily to encapsulate the slave trade. Failure to recognize that the status quo was not good just because it was there would have meant that we would still be degrading human beings by buying and selling them. The position with assisted suicide is not dissimilar. Social change will naturally follow from its legalization, but to insist that this change will inevitably be for the bad is neither proved nor plausible.

In fact, it can be argued, with evidence to back it up, that the greater evil may result from a failure to legalize assisted death. As Logue says, under current societal rules, 'To die on their own terms, patients must act *before* they become too incapacitated. Hence individuals may be driven to end their lives prematurely, while they still can, lest their health declines to the point where it becomes impossible to implement their decision.'[4] This can scarcely be viewed as a 'good' outcome. Yet at the heart of the arguments against assisted death is the conviction that prohibiting it will result in more lives being lived to their 'natural' conclusion. Logue, however, would argue that this is every bit as likely a consequence of a legal system which permits aid in dying. She concludes, therefore, that 'It follows that if people were confident that help would be available when and if it was needed they would undoubtedly choose to live longer; moreover, the quality of their remaining time might well be improved as their fears of helplessness subside.'[5]

Of course, nobody can prove that this is the case – for some it may even be counter-intuitive. And intuition, as we have shown, plays a very large, albeit unspoken role in the arguments against assisted death. When rationally considered, the flaws in the arguments against legalization of assisted suicide largely become obvious when the leap between argument and intuition is institutionalized into them. For reasons such as these, the slippery slope argument doesn't work. In any event, Rachels exhorts us to be cautious about intuitions.

He says, 'The idea is always to be suspicious of them, and to rely on as few of them as possible; only after examining them critically, and only after pushing the arguments and explanations as far as they will go without them. Every concession to intuition is just that – a concession. The complaint about the intuitions underlying the traditional approach is, in the end, not that they are intuitions, but that they are intuitions trusted too easily.'[6]

Equally, they can be intuitions – or assertions – which are not morally cogent when analysed. For example, in declining to recommend a change in the law in respect of euthanasia, the House of Lords Select Committee on Medical Ethics (UK)[7] concluded that '... dying is not only a personal or individual affair. The death of a person affects the lives of others, often in ways and to an extent which cannot be foreseen. We believe that the issue of euthanasia is one in which the interest of the individual cannot be separated from the interest of society as a whole.'[8]

In this statement we see the classic move from provable assertion to intuition disguised as logic which colours much of this debate. Manifestly, an individual's death affects others, but this is true **no matter how that person dies**. Certain kinds of death, for example as the result of murder or accident, may shock more, but the loss remains the same. In fact, a death which follows unrelieved suffering and repeated requests for assistance which cannot legally be met might result in similar levels of shock for those who must witness it. Thus, the first part of the statement from the House of Lords is rooted in reality, even if it does not take that reality far enough. It is a mantra rather than a whole truth.

But then comes intuition. With no argument, intellectual or moral, euthanasia and, logically, assisted suicide are singled out as being intimately linked to the 'interest of society as a whole'. Does this mean that other deaths are not? Of course it doesn't, and the House of Lords has already conceded this. What it means is that

presumptions, presuppositions and personal prejudices have
been allowed to predict a conclusion which is both unjustified and
unjustifiable. Society might equally be said to have an interest in
ensuring that people are able to vindicate their freely expressed and
freely taken choices about their own deaths. Certainly, society has an
interest in protecting people from being killed, but this is fundamentally
different from preventing people from exercising their own individual
choice to die. Intuition, however, has been elevated in this view to the
level of dogma.

Their Lordships must surely be right that the interests of the
individual and those of society are, as Dougherty[9] also argues,
inextricably linked in this as in other areas, but what they – and those
who think like them – do not explain is on what basis they presume
to know which outcome actually serves the interests of the community.
Indeed, there is something profoundly paradoxical about their
conclusions on euthanasia and assisted suicide, given that they see
no difficulty about encouraging the making of advance statements
refusing life-sustaining treatment, they uphold the right not to
commence treatment, and their judicial body has allowed the removal
of nutrition and hydration from individuals in persistent vegetative
state who have had no opportunity of declaring their interest with
the sole and expressed intention of causing their death.[10] It is by no
means unarguable that these deaths can or should be separated from
the interests of the community, and by no means obvious why the
consequences of permitting these deaths should be better than those
which would flow from permitting people to make their own, sane
and contemporaneous, decision about death.

In reality, these examples show that the community already
accepts that some deaths are preferable to, or at least no worse than,
some lives. For Rachels and other commentators, the fact that it is
not wrong to kill oneself implies logically that it is not wrong to ask
someone for help when suicide cannot be achieved independently. It

might be wrong to **force** the third party to assist, but it cannot be wrong to ask. Our evidence, and that of other studies, shows that some people are willing to accede to the request, and that others might do so if it were not against the law. Their autonomy too is vindicated by allowing them to do what they feel to be the best and the most compassionate thing for their patient. In any event, as has been said, 'We think that killing is worse than letting die because, to some extent, we overestimate how bad it is to kill.'[11]

For the moment, it must be conceded, the onus is on those who wish to see a change in the law to prove their case. This is the general rule of argument. We believe that we have succeeded in significantly weakening the arguments against physician assisted suicide and welcome the response of its opponents, not least because the status quo is not based on any evidence that what society is doing currently is good, and that what society is prohibiting is bad. Indeed, hopefully our argument will encourage those who oppose legalization to address their own rationale for this. As Wildes says: 'The availability of assisted suicide and euthanasia will force those with moral convictions opposed to these practices to develop accounts of which kinds of collaboration are licit, why, and when. Moreover, these accounts must be articulated in general secular terms if they are to help avoid significant misunderstandings amongst those with divergent moral viewpoints.'[12]

Meantime, however, we are forced to live with the paradox that other people may reach conclusions about our lives (and more importantly, perhaps, our deaths) which are then acted upon by doctors, whilst we may not ask them to act on our **own** choice without rendering doctors guilty of a criminal offence. The ultimate outcomes of this situation are cruelty and discrimination – scarcely goals to be striven for. The cruelty is associated with turning our own desire for life, our own arguable convictions about consequences, into an argument which forces life on people who no longer wish it. It results in the situations described throughout this book – the pitiful and distressing stories which accompany people's efforts for legal recognition of their right to manage and control their own deaths. Shavelson's[13] account of the death of his friend by overdose cannot but tug at the heart strings:

Mary put one of the Secanol tablets in her mouth at a time, then swallowed it with a few gulps of water. Within a few minutes, she had taken nearly all thirty capsules, with a cup-and-a-half of water. When she placed the final pill in her mouth she looked at me, nodded, and swallowed it down. Then she lay back on the pillow and stared straight ahead, waiting. For ten minutes, Mary said nothing. The suddenly, 'I'm going to throw up.' Mary's voice was calm, but her face showed the panic. She began to repeat, sternly, 'I will not vomit, I cannot vomit.' But her body was racked with a single convulsive movement as her stomach contracted, propelling its contents upwards. I grabbed a basin and held it in front of her. Mary's hand held my wrist, her grip tight and desperate as she clenched her teeth together to keep the vomit in her mouth from coming out. Then she closed her eyes, tilted her head, and swallowed the pills back down ... Two hours later she was dead.[14]

Can anyone reading this doubt that Mary meant to die? Can anyone say that her death was a good one? With qualified assistance her real and enduring decision could have been respected without forcing her to swallow her own vomit. Mary's death was wanted, but it was not pleasant. But in some ways she was lucky – unlike many suicides, she was not alone, forced to hide for fear of being talked out of what she so clearly wanted or for fear of rendering someone else complicit in her death. Only very compelling reasons would render what she was forced to do anything other than barbaric, and, we have argued, these reasons do not exist.

If one of medicine's goals is to alleviate suffering and help people to die with comfort and dignity, then failure to allow doctors to help avoid situations like the one in which Mary found herself is both a denial of the aims of medicine and a reduction of people's last moments to terror, panic and discomfort.

On the question of discrimination, it is also clear that some may achieve their good death while others cannot, largely because of the so-called 'distinction' which is the acts/omissions doctrine. A decision for death is unlikely to be an easy one, but once made it is allowed in some cases and not in others. Its rationale is irrelevant in some cases but closely analysed in those where the outcome requires active assistance. There is no clear argument in ethics or in rationality why this should be so, and therefore no justification for the law to collude in perpetuating it. The call for the legalization of physician assisted suicide is based on a set of values which are both consistent and clear. Legalizing assisted suicide will not make the choice for death any easier. As Mayo and Gunderson say: 'Since few persons will desire death as a positive good, legalization will rarely make a hard decision easy. However, it will add the new option of physician assisted death, which some will choose as the least onerous alternative in a hard choice.'[15]

Their argument, which would create equivalence between those who currently can choose death and those who cannot, concedes that legalizing assisted suicide may cause moral dilemmas. However, they conclude that: 'In those cases in which legalization simply adds a new option to the original hard choice while leaving all previous options intact, the person is not harmed, and legalization provides no reason for alleviating the resulting hard choice, even though the least onerous option is death. In those cases in which legalization does worsen the hard choice, however, legalization will provide reasons, although not necessarily conclusive reasons, for adopting safeguards, to ensure that these hard choices are not made even harder.'[16]

It is clear that attitudes to self-destruction have varied over the centuries. To some it may seem paradoxical that in a world where, at least in the developed countries, we can look forward to longer lives, the debate about choosing our own death should have taken on such momentum. Science is offering us life extension – why would we seek self-destruction? The answer is not hard to find. Longer life is not necessarily better life. A better death, chosen, controlled and comfortable, might imply a better life. As Erasmus said: 'No one has died miserably who has lived well.' The knowledge that our death could be a reflection of the values, principles and convictions which are personal to us may help to shape that life lived well and remove some of the fears of death itself.

In the poignant words of Daniel Callahan: 'The power of medicine to extend life under poor circumstances is now widely and increasingly feared. The combined powers of a quasi-religious tradition of respect for individual life and a secular tradition of relentless medical progress, creates a bias towards aggressive, often unremitting treatment that appears unstoppable.'[17] It is the fear of this 'relentless', some would say inhumane, juggernaut that has led to the frequency of calls for legal change.

The arguments, historical and analytical, demonstrate that social and legal progress can eventually result from changes in perceptions and in circumstances. It is little surprise that, given the advances in medicine and the increasing domination of rights-based arguments, the move for a say in the manner and timing of one's own death has become one of the major social forces of recent years. Even some judges have taken this on board. In the US case of *Bouvia* v. *Superior Court*[18], Compton, J. had this to say:

The right to die is an integral part of our right to control our own destinies so long as the rights of others are not affected. That right should, in my opinion, include the ability to enlist assistance from others, including the medical profession, in making death as painless and quick as possible.[19]

This is all that the argument in this book seeks to achieve. Peeling away the layers of those arguments which would militate against assisted suicide, it becomes clear that few, if any of them can trump those in favour. A society which condemns people to die like Mary or like Sue Rodriguez is a society high on pious rhetoric and low on compassion. Its claims to civilization are in doubt when it condemns the most helpless to dying disenfranchised and in despair.

Notes

Chapter 1: Why Not Assisted Suicide?

1   Biggs, H. and Diesfeld, K., 'Assisted suicide for people with
    depression: an advocate's perspective', *Medical Law International* 2.23
    (1995): 25

2   For discussion, see Rupp, M. T. and Isenhower, H. L., 'Pharmacists'
    attitudes toward physician-assisted suicide', Reports, *American Journal
    of Hospital Pharmacology* 51 (January 1, 1994): 69

3   Biggs and Diesfeld: 26

4   Osgood, N., 'Assisted Suicide and Older People: A Deadly
    Combination: Ethical Problems in Permitting Assisted Suicide', *Issues
    in Law and Medicine* 10.4 (Spring 1995): 416

5   *Re T* (adult: Refusal of Treatment) [1992] 3 Med.L.R. 306

6   For example, *Re B* (a minor) (wardship: medical treatment) 1 WLR 1421

7   Giesen, D., 'Dilemmas at life's end: a comparative legal perspective',
    in Keown, J. (ed.), *Euthanasia Examined: Ethical, Clinical and Legal
    Perspectives* (Cambridge University Press, 1995): 213

8   CeloCruz, M. T., 'Aid-in-Dying: Should We Decriminalize Physician-Assisted Suicide and Physician-Committed Euthanasia?', *American Journal of Law and Medicine* XVIII.4 (1992): 388

9   Gillon, R., 'Euthanasia, withholding life-prolonging treatment and moral differences between killing and letting die', *Journal of Medical Ethics* 14 (1988): 115

10   House of Lords Select Committee on Medical Ethics (HL Paper 21-1; London: HMSO, 1994)

11   National Council for Hospice and Palliative Care Services, *Key Issues in Palliative Care: Evidence to the House of Lords Select Committee on Medical Ethics* (Occasional Paper 3, July 1993): 4

12   Reno, J., 'A Little Help From My Friends: The Legal Status of Assisted Suicide', *Creighton Law Review* 25 (1992): 1151

13   Reno: 1158

14   Glover, J., *Causing Death and Saving Lives* (Penguin, 1984)

15   *see Note 9, above*

16   Miller, J., *The Body in Question* (Bookclub Associates by arrangement with Jonathan Cape Ltd., 1980): 244

17   National Council for Hospice and Palliative Care Services: 14

18   National Council for Hospice and Palliative Care Services: 8

19   Shavelson, L., *A Chosen Death: The Dying Confront Assisted Suicide* (Simon and Schuster, 1995): 218

20   Seale, C. and Addington-Hall, J., 'Euthanasia: The Role of Good Care', *Journal of Social Science and Medicine* 40.5 (1995): 586

21   *Ibid.*

22   *Ibid.*

23   Seale and Addington-Hall: 587

24   Ubel, P. A., 'Assisted Suicide and the Case of Dr Quill and Diane', *Issues in Law and Medicine* 8.4 (Spring 1993): 498

25   Koehn, D., *The Ground of Professional Ethics* (Routledge, 1994): 38

26   Wesley, P., 'Dying Safely', *Issues in Law and Medicine* 8.4 (Spring 1993): 467

NOTES

27   Wesley: 482

28   Wesley: 484

29   Osgood, N. J. and Eisenhandler, S. A., 'Gender and Assisted and Acquiescent Suicide: A Suicidologist's Perspective', *Issues in Law and Medicine* 9.4 (Spring 1994): 361

30   Osgood and Eisenhandler: 364

31   *Ibid.*

32   Angell, M., 'Prisoners of Technology: The Case of Nancy Cruzan', *New England Journal of Medicine* 322 (1990): 1228

33   Miller, P. S., 'The Impact of Assisted Suicide on Persons with Disabilities – Is It A Right Without Freedom?' *Issues in Law and Medicine* 9.1 (Summer 1993): 47

34   Miller, P.S.: 48

35   *Ibid.*

36   National Council for Hospice and Palliative Care Services: 4

37   National Council for Hospice and Palliative Care Services: 13

38   Beauchamp, T. L. and Childress, J. S., *Principles of Biomedical Ethics* (4th edn; Oxford University Press, 1994)

39   Beauchamp and Childress: 231

40   *Ibid.*

41   Giesen: 213

42   Giesen: 204

43   Weir, R. S., 'The Morality of Physician-Assisted Suicide', *Law, Medicine and Health Care* 20.1–2 (Spring/Summer 1992): 116

44   Weir: 122

45   CeloCruz: 383

46   Dworkin, R., 'When is it Right to Die?', *Last Rights* 12 (Spring 1994): 10

47   *Ibid.*

Chapter 2: Claiming the Right to Aid in Dying

1   Rachels, J., At *The End of Life: Euthanasia and Morality* (Oxford University Press, 1986): 78

2   Beauchamp, T. L. and Childress, J. S., *Principles of Biomedical Ethics*
    (4th edn; Oxford University Press, 1994)

3   Beauchamp and Childress: 121

4   Katz, J., *The Silent World of Doctor and Patient* (New York: The Free Press,
    1982)

5   Katz: xvii

6   Kennedy, I., *Treat Me Right* (Clarendon Press, 1988): 325–6

7   (1990) 67 D.L.R. (4th) 321

8   *Bouvia* v. *Superior Court* 225 Cal.Reptr. 287 (Cl.App., 1986)

9   *Re C* 15 BMLR 77 (1993)

10 Brock, D., 'Death and Dying', in Veatch, R. M. (ed.), *Medical Ethics*
    (Boston: Jones and Bartlett Publishers, 1989): 345

11 Weir, R. S., 'The Morality of Physician-Assisted Suicide', *Law, Medicine
    and Health Care* 20.1–2 (Spring/Summer, 1992): 124

12 Brandt, R. B., 'The Morality and Rationality of Suicide' in Veatch, *op.cit.*

13 Brandt: 70

14 Beauchamp and Childress: 226

15 Brandt: 73

16 Battin, M., *The Least Worst Death: Essays in Bioethics on the End of Life*
    (Oxford University Press, 1994): 54

17 *Ibid.*

18 *Rodriguez* v. *A-G of British Columbia* [1993] 3 WWR 553

19 Pellegrino, E., 'Intersections of Western Biomedical Ethics and World
    Culture: Problematic and Possibility', *Cambridge Quarterly of Healthcare
    Ethics* 3 (1992): 193

20 Kennedy: 320

21 As quoted in Shavelson, L., *A Chosen Death: The Dying Confront Assisted
    Suicide* (Simon and Schuster, 1995): 231

22 Battin: 54

23 Battin: 55

24 *Ibid.*

25 Dworkin, R., 'When Is It Right To Die?' *New York Times*, May 5, 1994.

NOTES

26 Weir: 122
27 Callahan, D., *What kind of life: the limits of medical progress* (Simon and Schuster, 1990): 143
28 Koehn. D., *The Ground of Professional Ethics* (Routledge, 1994): 122
29 Shavelson: 216
30 As quoted in Rachels: 19
31 From John Donne, *Devotions*
32 Rachels: 24
33 Jecker, N. S. and Schneiderman, L. J., 'Medical Futility: The Duty Not To Treat', *Cambridge Quarterly of Healthcare Ethics* 2 (1993): 158
34 Battin: 42
35 Battin: 43
36 Kass, L. R., *Toward a More Natural Science: Biology and Human Affairs* (New York: The Free Press, 1985): 32
37 Knox, R. A., *The Boston Globe*, February 28, 1992
38 Beauchamp and Childress: 225
39 Shavelson: 103
40 Quill, T. E., Cassell, C. K. and Meier, D. E., 'Care of the Hopelessly Ill: Proposed Clinical Criteria for Physician-Assisted Suicide', *New England Journal of Medicine* 327: 1380
41 Weir: 122

Chapter 3: Death, Hippocrates and Medical Ethics

1 Clements, C., 'Systems Ethics and the History of medical Ethics', *Psychiatric Quarterly* 64 (1992): 367–90; Monmeyer, R., 'Does Physician Assisted Suicide Violate the Integrity of Medicine?' *The Journal of Medicine and Philosophy* 205 (1995): 13–24
2 Richter, J. W., *The Hippocratic Oath Revisited* (Durham: Pentland Press Ltd, 1994): 44
3 Clements: 367
4 Richter: 15
5 *Ibid.*

6   Cowley, L., *et al.*, 'Care of the dying: An ethical and historical
    perspective', *Critical Care Medicine* 10.20 (1992): 1475

7   Richter: 19–21

8   *Ibid*.

9   As described by Plato in Richter: 19–21

10 Richter: 20

11 King, L. S., *A History of Medicine* (Penguin, 1971) 39–40

12 Cowley: 1475

13 Richter: 21

14 Hippocrates, *Aphorisms* I; trans. in Margotta, R., *The Hamlyn History of
    Medicine* (Hamlyn, 1996)

15 Miller, J., *The Body in Question* (Bookclub Associates, 1980): 185, 225–6

16 Gaarder, J., *Sophie's World* (Phoenix, 1996): 47

17 Cowley: 1475

18 Cowley: 1476

19 Underwood, J. A. (trans.), *Franz Kafka Stories 1904–1924* (Abacus, 1995):
    186

20 Cowley: 1479

21 211 N.Y. 125, 105 N.E 92 (1914)

22 Callahan, D., *What Kind of Life: The Limits of Medical Progress* (Simon
    and Schuster, 1990): 25

23 Callahan: 23

24 Jones, W. H. S. (trans.), *Epidemics* 1:11 from *Hippocrates* (vol. 1;
    Cambridge, MA: Harvard University Press, 1923): 165

25 Beauchamp, L. and Childress, J. S., *Principles of Biomedical Ethics* (4th
    edn; Oxford University Press, 1994): 262–3

26 See, for example, the Abortion Act 1967 UK, as amended

27 Beauchamp and Childress: 189

28 Jones, W. H. S. (trans.), Hippocrates: The Art in *Hippocrates* (vol. 2;
    Cambridge, MA: Harvard University Press, 1959): 193

29 Alvarez, A., *The Background in Suicide: The Philosophical Issues*, in Battin,
    M., Pabst and Mayor, D., (Des) 1980: 18

30 Durkheim, E., *Suicide: A Study in Sociology* (trans. Spaulding and Simpson, 1951): 330

31 Battin, M. *The Least Worst Death: Essays in Bioethics on the End of Life* (Oxford University Press, 1994): 16

32 *Compassion in Dying v. Washington*, 49 F.3D 590, -F.3d-(en banc.9th Cir. 1996).; *Quill v. Vacco* F.3d-(2nd. Cir. 1996) No. 95-7028

33 Koehn, D., *The Ground of Professional Ethics* (Routledge, 1994): 76

34 Cowley: 1476, quoting from the *Prognostic*

35 Monmeyer: 19

36 *Ibid.*

37 Koehn: 123

38 Monmeyer: 18

39 Edelstein, L., *The Hippocratic Oath* (Baltimore: Johns Hopkins Press, 1943): 62

40 Burgess, M., 'The Medicalisation of Dying', *The Journal of Medicine and Philosophy* 18 (1993): 273

41 Battin: 219

Chapter 4: Why Doctors?

1 Griffiths, J., 'Recent Developments in the Netherlands Concerning Euthanasia and Other Medical Behaviour that Shortens Life' *Medical Law International* 1 (1995): 375

2 Thomasma, D., 'Freedom, Dependency, and the Care of the Very Old' *Journal of the American Geriatrics Society* 32.12: 908

3 This is a theme that has been explored by Capron, A., 'Legal and Ethical Problem in Decisions for Death', *Law, Medicine and Healthcare*, 14:3/4 (1986) 141

4 *Re Quinlan*, 355 A.2d 644(N.J.) 1976

5 *Ibid.*

6 *Re C (Adult: Refusal of Treatment)* [1994] 1 WLR 290

7 *Re T* [1992] 4 All ER 649

8 *Airedale NHS Trust v. Bland* [1993] 1 All ER 821

9   Ibid.

10 House of Lords Select Committee on Medical Ethics (HL Paper 21-1;
    London: HMSO, 1994)

11 British Medical Association, Advance Statements about Medical
    Treatment (BMJ Publishing, 1995)

12 British Medical Association: 3 (emphasis added)

13 British Medical Association: 2

14 891 7 Supp. 1429 (D.Oreg.1994)

15 Compassion in Dying v. Washington, 49 F.3d 590, -F.3d-(en banc.9th
    Cir. 1996)

16 Cruzan v. Director, Missouri Department of Health 110 S Ct 2841 (1990)

17 Planned Parenthood v. Casey 112 S Ct 2791 (1992)

18 Quill v. Vacco F.3d-(2nd. Cir. 1996) No. 95-7028

19 Palermo, G. B., 'Physician Assisted Suicide: A Merciful Felony or a Search
    for Lost Omnipotence?', Neurology Psychiatry Sci. Um 15.2 (1954): 319

Chapter 5: A Comparative Study

1   Quill v. Vacco F.3d-(2nd. Cir. 1996) No. 95-7028

2   For a full discussion, see Jecker, N., 'Physician Assisted Death in the
    Netherlands and the United States: Ethical and Cultural Aspects of
    Health Policy Development', JAGS 42 (1994): 673

3   Ibid.

4   Kadish, S. H., 'Letting Patients Die: Legal and Moral Reflections',
    California Law Review 80 (1992): 860

5   Risley, R., 'Voluntary Active Euthanasia: The Next Frontier, Impact on
    the Indigent', Issues in Law and Medicine 8.3 (Winter 1992): 365

6   Quill, T. E., 'Death and Dignity: A Case of Individualised
    Decisionmaking', New England Journal of Medicine 324 (1994): 691–4

7   Pugilese, J., 'Don't Ask – Don't Tell: The Secret Practice of Physician
    Assisted Suicide', Hastings Law Journal 44.1291 (1993): 1295

8   Kadish: 861

9   Quill, T. E., Cassell, C. K. and Meier, D. E., 'Care of the Hopelessly Ill:
     Proposed Clinical Criteria for Physician Assisted Suicide', *New England
     Journal of Medicine* 327: 1380–4

10   Jecker: 673

11   Nederlandse Jurisprudentie (N.J.) (1985) No. 106, 451 452

12   Hoge Raad, 21 June 1994, Strafkamer nr. 96.972

13   The book appeared as part no. 40 in *The Dutch Library of Medicine*

14   Staatscommissie Euthanasie. Rapport inzake euthanasie,
     Statsuitgeverij, den Haag, 1985

15   Hoge Raad, 21 June 1994, Strafkamer nr. 96.972

16   Griffiths, J., 'The Chabot Case', *Modern Law Review* 58.2 (1995): 253

17   Griffiths: 239

18   van der Maas, P. J., *et al.*, 'Euthanasia and other medical decisions
     concerning the end of life: an investigation performed upon request
     of the Commission of Inquiry into medical practice concerning
     Euthanasia', *Health Policy* 22 (1992; special issue)

19   van der Maas, P. J. *et al.* 'Euthanasia and other medical decisions
     concerning the end of life', *Lancet* 338 (1991): 669

20   La France, A. B, 'Physician Assisted Death: A Comparison of the
     Oregon and Northern Territory Statutes', Draft, June 1996: 7. Our
     thanks to Professor La France for the use of this draft which, to our
     knowledge, has not as yet been published.

21   Blendon, R. J., Szalay, U. S. and Knox, R. A., 'Should Physicians Aid
     Their Patients in Dying? The Public Perspective', *Journal of the
     American Medical Association* 267 (1992): 2658–62

22   Cassel, C., 'Doctors and Allocation Decisions: A new role in the new
     Medicare', *Journal of Health Policy Law* 10 (1985): 549–64

23   Admiraal, P., 'Voluntary Euthanasia: The Dutch Way', in McLean, S. A.
     M. (ed.), *Death, Dying and the Law* (Aldershot: Dartmouth, 1996)

24   Miles, S., Gomez, C., *Protocols for Elective Use of Life Sustaining Treatment*
     (New York: Springer-Verlag, 1988)

25   Battin, M., 'Euthanasia: The Way We Do It, the Way They Do It', *J. Pain Symptom Manage.* 6 (1991): 299
26   Admiraal
27   This was known as Initiative 119 and was defeated 54 per cent to 46 per cent
28   This was known as Initiative 161 and was defeated by the same percentage as above
29   *LACMA Physician*, Los Angeles, California, February 6 1995
30   *Trustee* May 1995 (Chicago, Illinois): 27
31   *Oncology Times* May 1995 (New York)
32   Smith, C., 1996 'Safeguards for Physician Assisted Suicide: The Oregon Death with Dignity Act', in McLean, S. A. M. (ed.), *Death, Dying and the Law* (Aldershot: Dartmouth, 1996)
33   Ref. no. 2768, July 1995
34   For example, a second chamber as exists in the US and UK
35   As defined by s3 of the Act
36   *The Herald* (Glasgow), 1st July 1996 (Glasgow)
37   British Medical Association, *News Review* September 1996: 23–5

Chapter 6: A Good Death

1   Dougherty, C. J., 'The Common Good, Terminal Illness and Euthanasia', *Issues in Law and Medicine* vol. 9, 2(1993): 151
2   Gunderson, M. and Mayo, D. J., 'Altruism and Physician Assisted Death', *The Journal of Medicine and Philosophy* 18 (1993): 285
3   Rachels, J., *At the End of Life: Euthanasia and Morality* (Oxford University Press, 1986): 117
4   Logue, B., 'Physician assisted suicide: social science perspective on international trends', in McLean, S. A. M. (ed.), *Death, Dying and the Law* (Aldershot: Dartmouth, 1996): 107
5   *Ibid.*
6   Rachels: 150

7   House of Lords Select Committee on Medical Ethics (HL Paper 21-1; London: HMSO, 1994)

8   House of Lords Select Committee on Medical Ethics: 48, para 237

9   Dougherty

10   *Airedale NHS Trust v. Bland* [1993] 1 All ER 859. For the Scottish equivalent, see *Law Hospital NHS Trust v. Lord Advocate and Others* 22nd March, 1996 (Court of Session, unreported)

11   Rachels: 134

12   Wildes, K., 'Conscience, Referral and Physician Assisted Suicide', *The Journal of Medicine and Philosophy* 18 (1993): 327

13   Shavelson, L., *A Chosen Death: The Dying Confront Assisted Suicide* (Simon and Schuster, 1995)

14   Shavelson: 222–3

15   Mayo, D. J. and Gunderson, M., 'Physician Assisted Death and Hard Choices', *The Journal of Medicine and Philosophy* 18 (1993): 329

16   Mayo and Gunderson: 338

17   Callahan, D., 'Can We Return Death to Disease?', *Hastings Center Report* 4 (Special Supplement Jan/Feb, 1989)

18   *Bouvia v. Superior Court* 225 Cal.Reptr. 287 (Cl.App., 1986)

19   Compton: 307